searching for sea glass

A story of finding, remerging, and fortifying Soul.

Roberta A. Pellant

First Edition

Copyright © 2023 Roberta A. Pellant

All rights reserved.

ISBN: 978-1-952725-27-2 (paperback)

No part of this book may be reproduced or transmitted in any form or by any means, electronic or mechanical, including photocopying, recording, or by an information storage and retrieval system—except by a reviewer who may quote brief passages in a review to be printed in a magazine, newspaper, or on the Web—without permission in writing from the publisher.

Design by Melissa Williams Design
mwbookdesign.com

Early Praise for *Searching for Sea Glass*

"Dr. Roberta Pellant's approach to healing and self-discovery is truly groundbreaking. As a professor of psychology, I have never encountered a more honest and relatable account of the healing journey using both traditional and alternative therapies." —*Dr. Sarah J., Professor of Psychology*

"This book is a beacon of hope in a world that can often feel overwhelming. As a someone who has overcome addiction, I highly recommend it to anyone seeking inner peace and a deeper connection with themselves." —*Tom B., Meditation Instructor*

"Dr. Pellant's book is a powerful reminder of the resilience of the human spirit. As a trauma therapist, I have witnessed the transformative power of her approach, and I highly recommend it to anyone seeking to heal from trauma." —*Samantha K., MSW*

"This book is a game-changer for anyone seeking to break free from limiting beliefs and find their true purpose in life. As a business coach, I highly recommend it to anyone looking to achieve greater success and fulfillment." —*David H., Certified Business Coach*

"Dr. Pellant's book is a must-read for anyone interested in the transformative power of alternative therapies. I have been studying plant medicines for over a decade now, and I was impressed by her willingness to embrace a variety of healing modalities in order to achieve wholeness and peace." —*Michael B., PhD., Psychedelic Researcher*

"As a nurse, I am constantly seeking new ways to help my patients on their healing journeys. Her honest and relatable story, combined with her toolkit for self-discovery, makes this a must-read for anyone looking to improve their mental and physical health." —*Maria R., RN*

"This book was a catalyst for me. As a C-level executive, I am constantly seeking new ways to improve myself, my employees, and my business. Her approach to embracing failure and rising to the next level of success truly resonated with me." —*John D., Owner, and CEO*

"I am blown away by the wisdom and authenticity in this book. As a life coach, I will definitely recommend it to my clients as a powerful tool for self-discovery and healing." —*Raj W., Transformation Coach*

Foreword by Jack Canfield

For years, researchers and scientists have been fascinated by the therapeutic potential of psychedelics. Recent research in the field has shown promising results for treating a range of mental health issues, including trauma, addictions, childhood wounding, self-worth, and limiting beliefs. As a bestselling author, motivational speaker, and founder of both the Foundation of Self-Esteem and the Transformational Leadership Council, I have always been interested in cutting-edge research on personal development and transformational healing. When I first heard about Bobby's half memoir and half self-help toolkit, Searching for Sea Glass, I was intrigued.

As I delved deeper into her story, I was struck by Bobby's courage and her willingness to confront her deepest wounds and fears. Her story is a powerful testament to the transformative power of self-awareness, self-acceptance, and self-love. Her memoir takes readers on a journey through her childhood into adulthood and shows how she used both traditional and non-traditional psychedelic modalities to heal her adolescent and self-esteem wounds.

What sets *Searching for Sea Glass* apart from other self-help books is Bobby's honest and authentic writing style. She does not shy away from the raw, vulnerable moments of her life, but instead shares them in a way that is both inspiring and relatable and provides readers with practical tools and insights to help them on their own healing journeys.

As an academic and businesswoman, Bobby brings a unique perspective to the growing fascination and studies that psychedelics play in the role of personal development and transformational healing. Her extensive background in consulting, entrepreneurship, and executive leadership coaching gives her a wealth of knowledge and experience to draw upon. She is a sought-after 1-on-1 coach and group workshop facilitator, helping people from all walks of life to achieve their highest potential to live a more fulfilling life.

Bobby's story is a powerful reminder that deep inner healing is possible, and that we all have the ability to transform our lives in meaningful ways. And as someone who has personally witnessed and experienced the transformative power of this type of inner work myself, I can say with confidence that this book is an invaluable resource for anyone looking to achieve greater health, happiness, and fulfillment. I highly recommend this book to anyone who is looking for inspiration, guidance, alternative therapies, and practical tools to support them on their own healing journey.

—Jack Canfield, Coauthor of the *Chicken Soup for the Soul*® series and *The Success Principles*™: *How to Get from Where You Are to Where You Want to Be*

To Stephen,

"Love is an untamed force. When we try to control it, it destroys us. When we try to imprison it, it enslaves us. When we try to understand it, it leaves us feeling lost and confused."

—Paulo Coelho

Truly, Madly, Deeply.

—B.

To my Sisters: Cathleen, Ellen, Lauren, and Lisa.
You see Soul. Love is all there is.

Clockwise from top right: Ellen, Bobby, Lauren, Lisa, and Cathleen (middle).
Photo Credit: Karina Love: Plugin Mind©

Table of Contents

Foreword by Jack Canfield v
Disclaimers xii
Preface xiv
I Want to Age Like Sea Glass© xviii
Flashback—CoUnting xx

PART I: Childhood and Adolescence 1
   The Fall: The Breaking 3
   Earliest Memory 3
   Growing Up 4
   Scattered Memories of Young Life 11
   Teenage Years and High School 17

PART II: Adulthood and Ego 33
   The Winter: Shattered Fragments 35
   Basic Training and Military 38
   First Love and Anxious Attachment 48
   Modeling and Prince 50
   Transitions and Other Jobs 54
   Marriage 59
   Children 65
   More Schooling 69
   Divorce 77
   Consulting and Entrepreneurship 79
   Brothers 91
   Dating After Divorce 94

PART III: Seeking Oneness with Soul 99
   The Spring:Picking Up the Pieces 101
   My Spiritual Quest and Deepak Chopra 102
   Finding Soul and Merging Back: Ayahuasca 107
   Awareness and Reclaiming of Reality 120
   My Chosen Family and Sisterhood 122
   Plant Medicine: Psilocybin and Santa Maria 123
   Animal Medicine: Kambô and Bufo 126

PART IV: Healing Toolkit 133
   The Summer: Kintsugi Repairing 135
   Quieting the Mind: Hapé, Mambe, and Tinctures 136
   Crystals and Chakra Balancing 141
   Breathwork, Meditation, and Spirit Animals 144
   Writing, Sage, and Palo Santo 149
   Full and New Moon Rituals and Cacao 152
   Shadow Work 154
   Anger, Grief, and Forgiveness 157
   Boundaries 161
   Failure and Rebirth TEDx Talk 163
   The Body: Supplementing, Detoxing, and Intermittent Fasting 167
   Oracle Cards, Angels, and Dreams 173
   Present and Past Life Regression 180

PART V: Wholeness, to be Continued 183
   Sovereignty 185
   Soul Remembrance 186
   Intuition 188
   Life Not Yet Lived and Choosing 190

Acknowledgements 193
About the Author 195
Resources 197

Disclaimers

This book is a memoir. This work depicts actual events in the life of the author as truthfully as recollection permits. To respect the privacy of some individuals, initials are used, some events have been compressed, and some dialogue has been recreated. In other cases, when recognition is warranted, legal names have been used.

FOR EDUCATIONAL AND INFORMATIONAL PURPOSES ONLY

The information provided in the following sections and this book is for educational and informational purposes only and solely as a self-help tool for your own use.

NOT MEDICAL, MENTAL HEALTH, OR RELIGIOUS ADVICE

I am not, nor am I holding myself out to be a medical doctor, physician, nurse, physician's assistant, advanced practice nurse, or any other medical professional ("Medical Provider"), psychiatrist, psychologist, therapist, counselor, or social worker ("Mental Health Provider'), registered dietician or licensed nutritionist, or member of the clergy. I am not giving health care, medical or nutritional therapy services, or attempting to diagnose, treat, prevent, or cure any physical, mental, or emotional issues. The information provided in the following sections and book is not intended to be a substitute for the professional medical advice, diagnosis, or treatment provided by your own Medical Provider or Mental Health Provider. Always seek the advice of you own Medical Provider and/or Mental Health Provider regarding any questions or concerns you have about your health, or any medications, herbs, or supplements you are currently taking and before embarking or implementing any modalities, psychedelics, foods, diets, tinctures, or teas that I talk about in the following sections and this book. Do not disregard medical advice or delay seeking medical advice because of information you have read in the following sections and this book. Do not start or stop taking any medications without speaking to your own Medical Provider or Mental Health Provider. The information provided in the following sections and this book has not been evaluated by the Food and Drug Administration.

If you suspect that you have a medical or mental health problem, contact your own Medical Provider or Mental Health Provider promptly. If you or someone you know is experiencing suicidal thoughts or a crisis, please reach out immediately and call the U.S. National Suicide Prevention Lifeline, a free 24-hour hotline, at 1.800.273.8255. If your issue is an emergency, call 911 or go to your nearest emergency room. Outside of the U.S., please call your nearest hospital or check this resource guide.

THIRD PARTY DISCLAIMER

All information regarding recommended books, authors, Spiritual leaders, websites, and other businesses in the following sections and in this book is provided in good faith, and I make no representation or warranty of any kind, expressed or implied, regarding the accuracy, adequacy, validity, reliability, availability, or completeness of any information regarding third party claims, products, services, or sites. I, under no circumstances, shall have any liability to you for any loss or damage of any kind incurred as a result of the information provided by these third parties. Your use and reliance of the information provided by third parties is solely at your own risk. I will not be party to, or in any way responsible for monitoring any transaction between you and third-party providers of products or services.

Preface

October 15th, 2015, 8:00 a.m., Popponesset Beach

(5 pieces of sea glass found) I've walked this beach hundreds of times. Yoga pants rolled up, Havaiana flip flops, windbreaker, and today a skull cap with the Patriots Championship logo plastered across the front. I am always looking down, scanning the sand during low tide, searching for what is now elusive beach glass. With little wind and the sun breaking from the clouds over the horizon, it hits me like a ton of bricks. Am I really searching for sea glass? Or am I looking to find something else? While the shiny tiny pieces of glass, mostly brown, some white or green, and rarely the dark blue piece, make me utterly and completely happy and grateful for the small things in life, I stop in my tracks, wondering if what I am searching for is to find myself. Find my happiness and contentment to love myself like I love walking on the beach. What would happen if I lifted my head up from the daily façade of being an entertaining, knowledgeable, energetic professor, consultant, and business woman trying like hell to keep it all together; and instead became a joyful, passionate Soul flowing with grace and ease, Love and Light, allowing the Universe to conspire with me and co-create for my highest and most purposeful good?

Last month I made $800 an hour. That sounds bad-like I sold my body. But it was worse; I sold "my soul" consulting for a larger business looking to be acquired. What is Soul? How do you define it? My definition is that Soul/Spirit/Sovereign/Energy/Spiritual Heart/Intuition are interchangeable. My belief is that some human Beings are Starseeds, Spiritual Souls from the creation of stars sent here to Earth to transform the world. Other humans are here to fulfill karmic cycles (i.e., lessons to be learned and then released) and each of us has specific human life lessons that we are supposed to accomplish.

I believe our Souls never die; they just regenerate into different forms. When we are not satisfying Souls' purpose, we lose a bit of it. By lose, I mean that a particular part of it becomes hidden from our consciousness, and we forget the mission of our birth. By accepting this money to do a job that I really did not intuitively want to do, meant that my business mind and ego were rejecting my Soul's destiny. When we are younger, without realizing the Why behind this Soul's journey, we remember what brings us joy, makes us happy, and the passion for creating and transforming. As we grow older, and familial and societal expectations are placed on us, bit by bit, Soul shrinks from memory, and the ego/monkey mind/confused state is strengthened. Some people never choose to seek the path of enlightenment and never remember even a fragment of their purpose. Others remember and start the quest to re-merge Soul back to Source and why we have been born in this world. The lucky Ones remember this early in their life, even though I am a bit late to this process, but it does not take away from my gratitude for discovering how to awaken. This is my story of how I finally learned to do this. Throughout this book, you will see the words, Soul, Self, Spirit, Source, Sisters, One, Others, Beings, Light, etc., sometimes capitalized. This is out of appreciation and realization that these words represent Higher energetic expanded awareness vibrations, not the human physical self.

Most of us wish our childhood or our upbringing were different somehow. Not me. I loved my life. My earliest memory, which I will share shortly, might not have been a memory but a story that I have made up from seeing a picture, or even something I hoped was true in my mind. I have never had a great memory. I blame it on studying for tests all my life. So much so that my short-term memory was used more than my long-term memory. It might also simply be the fact that I have so much going on in this brain that I just push things out of the way to make room for other data. So, dear reader, while some of the things that you will soon read might seem far-fetched to you, I can assure you that they are very real. If there is something that I have exaggerated, I can assure you it's to the best of my memory. But what's a memory but a truth for that person? I am happy that you have decided to join me on my continuing Soul journey. This book is about regaining Soul while searching for sea glass and other healing modalities. Here we go; let's open our dragon wings and fly.

I Want to Age Like Sea Glass©

"I want to age like sea glass. Smoothed by tides, not broken. I want the currents of life to toss me around, shake me up and leave me feeling washed clean. I want my hard edges to soften as the years pass—made not weak but supple. I want to ride the waves, go with the flow, feel the impact of the surging tides rolling in and out.

When I am thrown against the shore and caught between the rocks and a hard place, I want to rest there until I can find the strength to do what is next. Not stuck—just waiting, pondering, feeling what it feels like to pause. And when I am ready, I will catch a wave and let it carry me along to the next place that I am supposed to be.

I want to be picked up on occasion by an unsuspected soul and carried along—just for the connection, just for the sake of appreciation and wonder. And with each encounter, new possibilities of collaboration are presented, and new ideas are born.

I want to age like sea glass so that when people see the old woman I'll become, they'll embrace all that I am. They'll marvel at my exquisite nature, hold me gently in their hands, and be awed by my well-earned patina. Neither flashy nor dull, just a perfect luster. And they'll wonder, if just for a second, what it is exactly I am made of and how I got to this very here and now. And we'll both feel lucky to be in that perfectly right place at that profoundly right time.

I want to age like sea glass. I want to enjoy the journey and let my preciousness be, not in spite of the impacts of life, but because of them."

—Bernadette Noll

Flashback—Counting

Seven years ago, I was searching for sea glass. I was in a dark abyss, all the while trying to gather the fragments of Soul, piece by piece no matter how small- collecting them like a beggar collecting coins, trying to put myself back together after being shattered into a bazillion pieces.

There are scattered thoughts rushing through my head; the pain of losing a baby, the pain of abandonment in relationships, and the pain of marrying the wrong person. I NEED to heal. I need to forgive my dad and my mom. I need to talk to someone, anyone, maybe my brother Jon. I am pissed! I was not in control when I was younger. How could my parents do this to me? It's embarrassing, so embarrassing. They were so selfish. I never asked for this. How did my brothers feel about this? Do they have the same trauma around this as I do?

When did I become so angry? I think it was in my 18-year marriage. Angry that he possibly fathered another child. What type of man did I marry? Marriage: a cocoon of safety. I am messed up. Really messed up. Figuratively not literally, unless you include the ½ of Alprazolam I ingested an hour ago. I had so much sadness, and I was ruminating, not knowing how to fix everything. Everything I touch is a disaster. I have been called a narcissist more times than I can remember. Self-destructive as well. I burn more bridges and have blown up more relationships, both with men and friendships with women, than any person I know. I feel toxic. The pain is so deep it's unbearable. To want what I want, when I want it, is that selfish, or is that hopeful? Stupid. Picking up the pieces of my life (61 pieces). Searching like a crazy lady, crying, walking in the rain, cold, soaking wet, trying to literally see and pick up the sea glass pieces. Fog rolling in, not another person on the beach. Truly alone yet thanking God for finding piece after piece. Seagulls screeching, yelling at me, yet I am the one crying out for help, truly cathartic. A journey: do I stop looking as if I have found the ultimate peace today? Forgiveness.

Another rainy day (73 pieces today), soaked to the bone with wet glasses, I can't tell which is the rain and what are my tears. I am fogged up and unable to see clearly until the sun comes up. I see the rocky beach, which reminds me of my rocky life. (104, 421, 196, 87 pieces throughout the week). Bright, sunny, warm day. Quiet and beautiful first day of summer (2016 with everyone on the beach at 10:00 a.m. (37, 35, 108 more.) I'm jealous of everyone; stop picking up the pieces! I want to be whole; I don't want you to take my wholeness. These are the pieces of my life!

(66 pieces today.) Blowing and windy, sad tears once again in my eyes. (125 pieces) remembering the smell of hot dogs, sloppy joes, and potato chips in the church hall during a rare school lunch. How simple life was. Then the shame. My dad said I had "big lungs" after swimming underwater four lengths of a round pool, coming up for air. Why can't I breathe now?

(174 pieces.) Today I forgave my father. He had a choice. But I have to believe that people do the best they can do at the time. I think he felt betrayed, alone, depressed, helpless, and thought there were no other options. He did not realize how much or for how long living there would affect me for the rest of my life. Or at least until I forgave. Memories of my mom with her nails, baring her teeth, drunk on vodka, scratching at my father. Angry selfishness, living out of scarcity versus living out of abundance. (63 pieces.) Today I tried to understand what was going on with my mom and forgave her for making me feel like she didn't love me. I realized that she was so unhappy because of my dad's strong personality.

Second walk on the beach today. First love, D. older,

mean, pull towards, push away, emotionally unavailable, violent, hitting, yelling, screaming, police called, arrests on both sides at two separate times. He had no respect for me, and I had no respect for myself.

(50 pieces.) I am trying to reconcile the fact that J. saved me from the turmoil of my earlier relationships. He was calm, safe, loving, easy to manipulate, and financially secure. (36 pieces.) He was a financial plan and safety net, an infatuation and stability. I remember the attorney's letter coming in the mail and him signing away any and all rights if the baby was his and taking the $5 enclosed for return postage that cost .25 cents in 1989. (44 pieces.) I apologized to J. and K. and the baby for bullying him into marrying me, saying he was gay, shirking responsibility, and forcing myself and marriage onto him. I remember convincing him to tell her he liked men so she would go away. (40 pieces.) I remember eating peas straight off the vine in South Milwaukee in the sun, seeing their white flowers, and popping tar bubbles in the alley with my bare toes in the hot-humid summer heat.

(24, 17 pieces.) Very tough self-talk today. Talking and trying to convince myself that I am enough. I, by myself, with what I have and don't have, is okay. How I look, what I do for work, what I possess and how I act, for the most part, is okay but not great. (132 pieces.)

On March 18th, at Hull Beach (17 pieces.), I walked past a homeless man on the beach who looked like my father. I'm wearing blue colored glasses to see the glass pieces better. Yet am I failing to see who I am, what my faults are, and how I have contributed to this chaotic life I have created? The harder I searched for myself, the longer I walked, the more sea glass I found (216 is my record so far).

Another rainy, cold, and wet freezing day, yet with flip flops always and a skirt. (104 pieces.) Is my heart or head remembering how I would fantasize about K. losing the baby; (66 pieces) going through the timeline of events. (56 pieces.) Crying every day now. (46 pieces.) Pain.

It was Memorial Day, and there was now a parking fee

associated with parking in the lot near the beach. I needed to walk but I took a week's reprieve. (61 pieces.) With no hope, I was despondent, overwhelmed, and struggling. (49 pieces.) I always chased emotionally or physically unavailable men. It made me anxious, upset, crazy, insecure, angry, have no dignity, reckless, uncaring, stupid. (50 pieces.) I apologized and forgave myself for fighting against myself. I would fight and yet rarely flee under stress. (47,95,94,48 pieces.)

I chose to love me! (42 pieces.) I let it go. (12 pieces.) Shallow day today, and I was not concentrating at all. Hard day, healing for annulment. No judgment at all from Father N. Take focus off your pain and concentrate on God's mercy and forgiveness. (213, 176, 27 pieces.) Cel's candy, stealing penny candy, and being forced to admit it and give back the money. Buying cigarettes for my mom. Unfinished business with my family, my brother. Annulment explanation and writing complete. Sixteen pages of written pain. Five hours later, relieved (17 pieces), still forgiving me. (142, 37, 15, 38 pieces.)

Two months later July 2016. (20, 68 pieces.), HORRIBLE night last night, and I got super drunk! (75 pieces.)

(67,68,72,14,43,533,73,11,23,6 pieces.) The kindness of strangers is something I am so grateful for. (55,37,48,42,34, 63,17,19,1,15,1,139,165,147,885,55,35,39,68,50,40,73,48 ,33,94,6,15,81,213,65,74,96,37,96,36,48,42,21,20,68,53,6 3,10,15,68,21,12,44,81,75,32,53,67,308,292,101,38,59,60, 50,50,34,58,73 pieces.) I am not making up these numbers for my sanity; I am actually counting them.

It's been seven years since I have been on my daily walks on the beach looking for sea glass, counting obsessively, rereading these words, and I can feel my pain and realize just how bad the longing to unite with Soul really was.

Almost all stories of growth start with a quest of discovery, searching, and longing. I was living my life, and then one day, I tumbled hard, sliding down a mountain to the very bottom, deep in the darkest of the recess; rock bottom, as it is sometimes called. Some choose to live there, not summoning the strength or doing the hard work that it takes to climb back out. Others (who I like to think I am one) will scratch, crawl, and drag themselves through the mud after the fall to ascend to a higher magnificent peak, reveling in the sun shining on my face once again. I liken this trip to the seasons in a year. The first two parts of the book are about my life. Part 1 is the tumble from the mountain and is obviously the Fall. Part 2 is the cold, dreary Winter, and the deep crevasse after the fall. Parts 2 and 3 are about my healing journey. Part 3 is the upward climb, the Spring, where there is new life and growth. Part 4 is the glorious mountain summit, the Summer where I can see all things clearly and bask in Light. I have experienced this cyclic season several times in my lifetime. Now I am on the most majestic, ultimate, high-energy vibration apex, and finally able to write about my seasons.

PART I:
Childhood and Adolescence

The Fall: The Breaking

> "As a child I felt myself to be alone, and I still am, because I know things and must hint at things which others apparently know nothing of, and for the most part do not want to know. Loneliness does not come from having no people about one, but from being unable to communicate the things that seem important to oneself, or from holding certain views which others find inadmissible."
>
> —*Carl Jung*

Earliest Memory

1968 or thereabouts, South Milwaukee, Wisconsin

I am a young, blonde, thin girl, approximately two years old, looking up at the sky. My hand is very tiny, long pianist fingers holding my father's baseball mitt of a hand, and we are both watching an airplane with a stream of exhaust fly by. I point to it, not remembering if I can articulate the word plane, and then I look at my dad. I am safe, well cared for, loved, and very happy. My father was the first person who loved me and made me feel special. It would take me half of a century to feel that way again. It was at this moment I truly realized I was extraordinary, gifted, and different. But as this story will show you, I ended up living unconsciously in a desolate parched desert from the ages of 16–42. I was searching for answers, thinking I needed to be fixed.

Growing Up

> "Growing up is losing some illusions, in order to acquire others."
>
> —*Virginia Woolf*

I grew up in the mid-60s and 70s in South Milwaukee, Wisconsin, which at the time, consisted of average-income Polish and German immigrants who, like my Grandparents, worked hard to be able to afford their houses and own various local neighborhood businesses. My earliest childhood memories are of being surrounded by my family: my mom, dad, three younger brothers, and four sets of aunts and uncles, with dozens of cousins in the nearby cities. I wanted for nothing.

My father and mother were the youngest in their families, and their siblings would say both were spoiled, as is the case with most older children referring to the babies. My father always had a penchant for the finer things in life, which trickled down into how I was raised. I went to the private Catholic school a few blocks away because, according to him, it was a better education and more disciplined than public school.

We always had the newest model luxury car; my dad took great pride in his car. He would drive me around the neighborhood with its frosty air conditioning, leather seats, and powered windows—a big deal at the time! But an even bigger deal was that we were a two-car family. My mom also had her own car, which she used to drive back and forth to work. It was unusual that I had a nanny, a young girl who came into our house to take care of me when I was young. When I got older, my Grandmother, who lived with us, took over that role.

What really set us apart from other families was the fact that we belonged to the Yacht Club on Lake Michigan. We had a beautiful wooden powerboat; I think it was a Chris-Craft, but don't hold me to that memory. While I never realized that I came from a much higher income level than most, it was evident by my cousins and others making comments on how I was always dressed in designer clothes and the newest fashions, the fact that we vacationed every summer away from home—sometimes internationally, and that we were always getting to do things that most people weren't able to. Life was idyllic, but more importantly, I was happy, safe, and secure with who I was.

—Excerpted from Women Who Empower, 2020.

I imagine I felt like a miracle to both of my parents, as my mom had suffered several miscarriages in the 1960s. This was due to Rh factor incompatibility.[1] This happens when the mother is blood-typed negative, and she carries a baby that is positive. With the advent of the RhoGAM injection (to build up antibodies), Diethylstilbestrol (DES), a synthetic form of estrogen, and her undergoing a cervical cerclage, my mother was able to bring either her 4th or 5th baby to term, delivering a healthy baby girl, me. I don't know how much I weighed or how long I was. I guess at Trinity Memorial Hospital in Cudahy, Wisconsin; they did not record those things back then. My mother Darlene, wanted to name me Jera Lyn, but of course my father Robert wanted a namesake; thus, I was to be Roberta Ann, *Bobbi(e)* as a nickname. Ann was chosen because both of my Grandmothers were named Anna. I use italics on the word *Bobbi(e)* because my mom always used "*i*" at the end. Other family members, including my younger self, used "*ie*" until finally, Bobby became my preferred spelling in high school. Only my mom's side of the family calls me Bobby Ann, and when I used to get in trouble, I was always Roberta!

My parents were both the youngest in birth order and were somewhat older when I was born: my dad was 34, and

---

1. Danielsson, K. & Levine, B., MD (2022). *Did my miscarriage happen because I am RH negative?* Retrieved on February 6th, 2023, from: https://www.verywellfamily.com/can-being-rh-negative-cause-a-miscarriage-2371474

my mom was 29. I was revered and loved as a child, passed around to anyone of my seven Aunts or Uncles and numerous older cousins. My Light was so bright, and I was such a happy toddler that I made everyone laugh and smile. I was a natural entertainer and enjoyed being admired, doted on, and paid attention to. This would soon become a major issue for me later in life.

Since my paternal Grandmother, Anna, was Prussian (her family was from Poznan, which was in West Prussian but is now considered Poland), she lived with us in a downstairs apartment of our house. I never knew my Grandfather, Edward, as he passed away before I was born. Both had siblings, my Great Aunts and Uncles, and they had children that lived in the area. Based on our Eastern European heritage, holidays were decadent with smoked oysters on New Year's Eve or beef tartare with onions. Thanksgiving, Christmas, and Easter were always filled with family; more maternal cousins than you could count, vodka, sweets, and my favorite dessert, grasshoppers: which consisted of crème de menthe, a sweet green minty liqueur poured over ice cream. When the house was full of people, Grandma C. would yell at all of us kids to be quiet and stop running amok. But during quiet times, she could cross her legs and hold our hands while we sat on her foot and sing, "Hiya, hiya, hiya," to soothe us and then drop us unexpectedly on the floor to make us laugh. Good times!

My father had four siblings: my Aunt Esther, who was also my Godmother, married to Uncle Richie, who had three girls: Gail, Linda, and Marcia. My Uncle George married my Aunt Antenna (Ann), who did not have children and lived in Arizona. I only saw them when they came back to visit. My Uncle Gene married my Aunt Jo-Jo, who had one girl, Susie. They lived close to us, and I would remember always riding over there and knocking on their door for a Coke or some type of snack. Occasionally we'd surprise Aunt Jo-Jo who would have pink curlers in her hair along with her ever-present lit Pall Mall cigarette. To this day, I remember my Uncle Gene as a clone of my father: fun-loving, always smiling, a beer in his hand, telling stories. My Auntie Irene just celebrated her 96th (!) birthday. She is living in California and is always seen by me as so beautiful and glamorous; married my Uncle Lloyd, and adopted two children: Craig and Lisa. Uncle Lloyd passed away, and she later married my Uncle Tony. On a sad note, my cousin Craig whose car was found near local mountains, near a local campsite off Toolbox Springs, Garner Valley, CA disappeared around June 22nd, 2018, without a trace, and still has not been found. I am so happy that I was able to reconnect with him in CA in 2017. I love you, cousin!

On my mother's side of the family, my maternal Grandparents were primarily Swedish, with a hint of Norwegian on my Grandmother Anna's side. She had two siblings: my Great Uncle Harry, who died before I was born, and my Great Uncle Oscar, who I remember fondly. I would walk his trap line with him in northern Wisconsin as a little girl, talking to him the entire way until we came in for lunch. Grandma Anna married Grandpa Oscar, who was 16 years older, so he seemed *really* old to me at the time and had a thick Swedish accent. I remember him being truly kind and quiet, always wearing black Chuck Taylor high tops, shuffling his feet when he'd leave the house to chop more wood for the fire. I also remember his tattoos on both arms, which he got when he was a sailor in the Swedish Army. He would sing in Swedish to me while bouncing on both legs, which seemed to be the thing at that time! Grandpa R. had two other brothers: Axel and Sven who stayed in Sweden, and I never met. He had some relatives in Thunder Bay, Canada, that we would travel to see every couple of years, but I lost track of them after I was married. My Grandma R. was always smiling, baking fresh bread that smelled delicious, watching her soap operas during the week, and always insisting on playing cards when we visited. When I got a little bit older, I remember her opening up her treasured cedar chests, which were full of old-fashioned fox stoles (head and all) and fine linens, presumably from Sweden, passed down to her from her mother.

My mom grew up with two sisters and a brother. My

Aunt Ginny married my Uncle Hits (Harold-we called him "Hits" because it was funny). They lived a few towns from us and had five children: Gary, Russ, Larry, Joe, and Linda. All these 1st cousins had several children as well, who ended up having kids, and many of them are still in the area. Her other sister Aunt Vi married my Uncle Gene (yes, another one), a half-blooded Chippewa or Ojibwe Native American Indian, who was my Godfather. They also lived very close and had seven children: Mike, Shirley, Doug, Kay-Kay, Butch, Tony, and Kenny. Because my dad hunted and fished with this Uncle Gene up North, I remember hanging out at their house and playing with the younger kids the most. Uncle Dick was married to Aunt Grace who was Dutch, and they had one daughter Anna. As with my father's side of the family, there is also a tragedy associated on my mom's side. When I was little, Uncle Dick was killed in Texas at their house; he was stabbed in the stomach and did not survive. My memory is that my Grandma Roos seemed to think it was because he was an accountant working on the books for an A&W franchise, and he found something; therefore, he was murdered. However, an investigation could not substantiate another person being involved, so therefore, I believe it was ruled that he had taken his own life. Aunt Grace later remarried Vern, and they had Eric, who I only met a few times. I remember the first time Grace and Vern came to our house in South Milwaukee in the early 70s. It was the first time that I met or even knew a Black person, but I was so proud of my parents, my dad especially, for telling me that he was family and skin color meant nothing.

When I was five years old, my brothers Jim and Jon were born, twins born extremely prematurely. I remember they were born in February and came home from the hospital in June. Needless to say, my mom was quite busy with them. So to keep me entertained and out of her hair, I was whisked away by my dad to do things together. Looking back during this time, I began to live my life for someone else, wanting his approval and seeking out male affection and attention.

Dear Mom,

I want you to know that I see you in me. Both of us ignored by the man/men in our lives, battling our own unheard, unachieved dreams due to an overbearing, selfish husband/ partner. How did it feel having a daughter who ignored her and was embarrassed by her- I took your husband from you- I understand your resentment and, to some extent, jealousy. Your dreams, ambition, motivation, and beauty were compromised the day you married my father. He knew it as well, and that's why I had such an unhealthy relationship-bond with him. I took the place of you in his life as a girl/child wife. I am sorry, I was just a child.

Love, Bobby

Knowing this, I also know that I was an unmothered child. I was not taught to cook, dress, do laundry, or learn about my sexuality from a woman. I had to acquire these skills on my own, learning and figuring it out myself or modeling the behavior from others, friends, or from what I saw on TV. I learned by doing it. If I failed or was ridiculed, I learned by trying again. I was never taught to live by Spirit or Instinctual Self. How could I, as a Divine feminine, being raised primarily by a masculine?

I always knew I was unique, not only from the attention and admiration I received but also because people told me I was beautiful, daring, smart, and charming. In other words, precocious. I don't say this conceitedly, but as a child I felt such overwhelming love and joy. I also knew I was special in other ways, and those gifts will be interwoven into this story.

The first time I felt remarkably beautiful was when I was 4 or 5 years old. My cousin was getting married, and I was to be the flower girl. I had my first manicure at the beauty salon, and my long blond hair was styled up in a bun with ringlets framing my face. I wore a satiny peach long dress, short white gloves, and a headband with a small bow and little veil. The flowers I carried were white daisies stuck into a round Styrofoam ball hanging from a white plastic chain. It was the prettiest thing I had ever seen. Everyone commented on how I looked, and I received so much attention and admiration that day.

My first recollection of being a Sacred rebel, without looking at a picture or a newspaper clipping, would have to be my first day of kindergarten. I met a friend named Julie. Somehow she caught my attention or smiled at me. She was my first friend besides my cousins. In those days, there was a Catholic school with a Church on practically every corner. There was no school lunch, so it was assumed we would walk home, have lunch, and return to school in the afternoon. Well, while talking to my new friend, I convinced her that I should eat lunch at her house that day. So I walked home with Julie, met her mom and other siblings, had my lunch, and walked back to school. Imagine my surprise when I was called to the principal's office, Sister Mary Christina, on the first day of school! My father, or babysitter at the time, must have called frantically, wondering where I was. I don't remember getting in too much trouble that time, only a stern talking to from my father. I spent seven years at that school, only having one nun, Sister Mary Dulcius, my teacher for first grade. In all my other classes, I had lay (non-religious or vowed) teachers. Lay teachers were just starting to infiltrate the Catholic schools. It was a big deal when there was a male teacher in 3rd grade. Also, something that might be unique about my grade school years is that I had no less than three cousins in my classes.

The second time I knew I was Spiritually open was two years later, in 2nd grade. I must have been around seven years old and I was making my 1st reconciliation. I had religion that was taught every day in school. Part of the process was for me to meet with a priest face to face in the church pews to ask him any questions and for him to help ease any nervousness I might have had. I vaguely remember talking to him about Souls. But what is crystal clear is when I asked him, "What happens to the animals when they die? Do they go to heaven too?" The priest said back to me with somewhat of a shocked look on his face, "Animals don't have Souls." I remember telling him that he didn't know that for sure, he wasn't God, and starting my first philosophical Spiritual debate! In my young mind, as I walked away from the conversation thinking that the priest didn't know what he was talking about. God would not deny anyone into Heaven. It wasn't until many years later when I started questioning the decisions of the Catholic Church, and seeking out other religious dogmas, that I remembered this conversation from so many years ago.

Scattered Memories of Young Life

> "Wasn't it beautiful when you believed in everything, and everybody believed in you?"
>
> —*Taylor Swift*

I can't remember much of the first 12 years of my life, and if I am being honest, not much after that either. I remember watching an old, reeled tape movie of my father carrying me down a steep flight of outdoor stairs to the waiting family in the yard below. As I watched, my father stumbled and dropped the "baby" (which was me) over the railing, and everyone screamed in alarm and my Uncle Gene, my dad's brother, ran to catch it. Everyone gasped, and my Grandma C. clutched at her heart, only to discover that inside the bundle, there was a doll. I was sleeping safe and sound inside, oblivious to anything happening. That was their way as brothers to pull a prank on everyone, but mostly my Grandmother.

I do remember having Scandinavian white-blond hair. I wanted it to be long and used a yellow cashmere scarf to attain that. I also recall being adored by my father and also by strangers. I remember having my picture taken and being in the South Milwaukee journal, what seemed like weekly. Once for eating pancakes at a church breakfast. I remember being content and fitting in, looking like everyone else in my uniform, albeit with Buster Brown custom-made saddle shoes because I had such a narrow foot and heel. I remember going to the local bakery after church, and picking up poppy seed horned rolls, belonging to the Yacht Club, my dad's boat, having "lollies"(lollipops) after a boat ride in the bar, the smell of fish rotting on Lake Michigan's beach, anchoring far out, and having to swim to the shore. I remember there were two cherry trees in the side yard in South Milwaukee, until a winter storm came, and one fell over. I remember the birds eating the sour cherries and me picking them from the tree for my mom to make a sweet jam. I remember my above ground swimming pool, tiger lilies, bright red poppies and brightly colored peonies, along with teeny purple violets alongside the house. The lilac bushes separating our house from the neighbors with their fragrant scent. I have one memory of my dad bringing a bunny rabbit home. Then one rainy day, while taking him to school for show and tell, I dropped the box he was being raised in. Then that same week, I watched a cat carry him in his mouth, walk down the alley, and me running to kick the cat. I was full of anger and sadness, knowing that I caused a life to be lost. I remember one 4th of July, my dad climbed up on the garage roof to throw M80s and firecrackers into the neighbor's lawn as a joke while they hosted a BBQ. But because he had a few vodkas, could not climb down the ladder, so the fire department had to be called. I remember seeing a cutout from the newspaper of my Grandma C. taking my Easter basket and turning it upside down, decorating it and wearing it on her head as an Easter bonnet, and winning the Easter bonnet contest. I remember Skipper, her mean dog who smelled like pee because he peed on everything. I remember riding my bike everywhere to meet friends or cousins, starting out when I first woke up and only coming home when it got dark out. I remember popping tar bubbles in the alleyway and not being able to wash the black sticky mess off my big toes, but I would go out during the hot summer midday and do it all over again. I remember car rides and walks around Grant Park with my dad until the day our fairly new car was stolen. Then we hitchhiked home, being picked up by a nice young man who would be called a hippie back then. Once home, I wanted to go back out to help my dad find the thieves, but more importantly, to find my purple Tootsie Roll Pop and some other school papers that were left in the car.

I have memories of sweet peas in our garden, next to our off-brand silver Airstream trailer and a smaller trailer duck hunting boat. My neighbor friend, Robert, came over and I taught him how to hop and leap from seat to seat on that boat until he slipped, and there was blood all over. I screamed to my dad, and my dad scooped him up to bring him home, his white t-shirt stained with Robert's blood. I remember seeing Robert the next weekend with his head shaved and dark black stitches running across the length of his head. Memories of school yard rhymes with hand slapping and clapping, jump roping, and around the world four squares with a big red rubber ball. Kleenex on my head and uniform skirt touching the pew when we knelt at church, taking up the communion, my dad singing church hymns in his loud alto voice, winning prizes at school in first grade, as I was a favorite (This is only probably due to the fact that my father tithed a lot of money to the church).

It was during this time, early on, I remember having out-of-body experiences. I am lying in bed, trying to fall asleep, drifting off into that place out of consciousness, and being lifted out of my body and hovering up over myself, looking at myself from above. I was at peace, in the stillness, floating. Whenever I could not fall asleep, I tried to get back to that experience. I remember it was my go-to sleep remedy for many, many years. This was the first time I realized I had my wings. During those younger years, I had a playful, wild Spirit, I was trusting of everyone I came in contact with, Soul was complete, and in some ways, I was deeply intuitive and knew my purpose for this life on Earth.

When I was younger, it seemed like it was a different world back then. We would leave the house first thing in the morning, on our bikes and not come home until dinnertime or until it was dark. I had a few close friends: there were only 20 in my primary K-7 classes, and three of which were my second cousins (Debbie, Marty, Chris). St. Adalbert's school and church were post-Vatican II, but it was very reluctant to change. We grew up with Masses in Latin and attended church seven days a week, Mass five days a week before class, confession on Saturdays, and then Mass on Sunday with family. Religion was such an important part of my upbringing. It was a simple, easy, carefree life. Sundays consisted of family dinners with our large extended family.

Hanging out with friends, we would ride our bikes to the creek, drag for crawfish and bring them back to my friend Julie's house for her mom to boil. While it was fun, I hated getting leeches on my legs, and we would carry salt with us whenever we went on this outing, to burn the leeches off our bodies. Also, at the public pool before you were allowed in through the turnstile to swim, we made sure we had our white plastic swim caps, complete with a chin strap, to prevent our long hair from getting into the pool drain. Everyone had to take a shower to rinse off before entering, and the final check was that we had to spread our toes on a bench to check for the athlete's foot. Imagine having that job!

While my earliest trip was at two years old on a plane to California, I don't remember apparently walking up and down the aisles and being tended to by the flight attendants. I remember driving eight hours north to Gordon, WI to visit my maternal Grandparents. My father was deer hunting, and we spent most Thanksgivings up there. I also remember waking up really early with my dad to drive our small boat and sometimes trailer to go duck hunting at Rush Lake, WI: the smell of the marsh, the reeds full of cattails, and even the sound of the duck call that I was able to blow while sitting still in the cold in our duck blind. I remember learning how to trap shoot and going to stock car and drag racing at Hales Corners Speedway. Once when I was out with my dad and his friend George, fishing on Lake Michigan, I remember him catching something and reeling it in. Suddenly, the line went slack. When he rolled in the line, he stumbled back in shock having a small piece of a scalp with hair come up. I remember promptly calling the Coast Guard from the radio and waiting until they arrived. My father and George gave their statements, and then we high-tailed back to the bar at the Yacht Club for a few stiff ones. Or rather, they did!

I remember listening to the song Delta Dawn on the radio in the kitchen, which my mom always had on, dancing to Johnny Cash on the record playing (my father's favorite). When Cash said, "Bring me another glass of water while at Folsom State Prison," I would always run to get him one! I vaguely remember the smell of my Uncle Gene C.'s pipe. The stronger memory, however, is the smell of my Uncle Gene K.'s cigar smoke, which I loved and still love to this day. I remember my Grandma C. making raisin toast with cream cheese and jelly on it for a snack for me, and never getting enough of it. Also, I can't forget my father's Russian Cossack lamb's wool winter hat and rubber slip-on over the shoe galoshes when he was dressing up in the winter to go to church.

I remember when we became a family of six. My mom was pregnant, and of course, I wanted a baby sister. My birthday, June 23rd, came and went without the usual fanfare or even one present. How dare they! I was mad. They forgot about me. I probably gave everyone the silent treatment, which to them was no doubt a relief. Ha! Around a week after my actual birthday, my father came home and said, "Happy Birthday, you have a baby brother," and it just cemented my anger and disappointment (sorry Mike). But then my dad promptly walked back outside and returned to present me with a large bird cage with a beautiful green parakeet in it. I named him Tweety, original, I know. This did temper my anger and help me forget about getting yet a third brother. Tweety used to open the door of his cage, get out and fly around the house, pooping all over the place, and stressing everyone out while we all screamed and tried to catch him. Except for my mom, who later I found out was afraid of birds. I loved that bird for several years. Until the day when he was put outside on the porch for the weekly cleaning, and he undid the bread tie wrapped around his cage door and flew away. Ahh, the thing about memories is that they are happy yet bittersweet at the same time.

I was wildly indulged. Always being treated a bit delicately and coddled-little Roberta. I was dressed up in the best clothes money could buy when my cousins ran around in hand-me-downs, ripped cut-off shorts, and white tee shirts. I remember crying at Christmas and my father going to the hallway to find that one last present they might have returned, except they didn't because of my spoiled-ness. The gift was sterling silver bird earrings. I was cognizant of having more material things than most: a larger house with a double lot, a beautiful boat with a sleeping cabin, taking family vacations up North, a silver camper parked next to our large garden, and an above-ground swimming pool. Yet, this was home to me. I had no care in the world. I followed the rules only when they pertained to me, or when they were easy to do so. Even then, I was a hypocrite. I held people to a higher standard than I did myself. On the outside I was charming, confident, rude, outgoing, judgmental, selfish, and sophisticated. I was a happy child, a rebellious child, and a spoiled child always going against the grain. A child who was sheltered from bad things that happen in life. Until I wasn't . . .

Teenage Years and High School

"I tried for so long to be all things to all people.
A chameleon of sorts, while slowing, shrinking, and eroding Spirit and Soul."
—Me

"It takes courage to grow up and become who you really are."
—E. E. Cummings

Then it all started to change, and my world was shaken to the core. It was the fall of 1976, and I had just finished the 7th grade. My paternal Grandmother had died at 81 years old. Right before this happened, my father had refused to pay his Teamsters Union dues and subsequently just lost his job. The three-story, 4-bedroom house I had known all my life, was now being sold because my father was battling with his siblings as there was no will when my Grandmother died, and we couldn't afford to live there any longer. Things were sold, packed up, and put in storage at one of my aunts and uncle's house because my parents couldn't even afford to pay for a storage unit. In the blink of an eye, how quickly things had changed. My mother was quiet. My father was devastated. Me, I didn't know what to think. I begged and pleaded to please let me stay in the city where my whole life was, but no. We were on our way to live on the same land as my maternal Grandmother in the Northwoods.

My new home in rural northern Wisconsin consisted of a three-room, not three bedrooms, but three-room, hunting cabin in the Northwoods. Room one was an open kitchen and dining room area, approximately 9 feet wide by 15 feet long. It consisted of the kitchen, a table with six chairs, a lounge chair for my dad to watch an old black and white small tv, a hutch for dishes and a gas-vented heater. The other two rooms were 9 feet wide by 7.5 feet long; one was my parents' bedroom, and my bedroom held double bunk beds that I shared with my three younger brothers. Do you see what was missing? A bathroom. Not only that, but this cabin did not have ANY running water in it. Fresh water would come from the pump house and be brought in by buckets to be heated for cooking and dishwashing, Little House of the Prairie style. This is not how I anticipated the start of my soon-to-be high school years, or how I would be living in the 80s!

It was soon September. Public school in Minong had already started, but I didn't enroll in time to start with the other students and did not get to pick my classes. I remember not having new clothes that first day but being thrilled to wear Levi orange tag jeans and Asics tennis shoes. What top to wear though? Nothing seemed right. After hours of agonizing over what to wear, my 88-year-old Grandma R. finally gave me a rose-colored, very dated sweater to borrow. Well, at least it was something. I walked into the classroom: long blonde hair, crooked buck teeth, cocky as all get out, a statuesque 5' 9 ½ inches weighing merely 120 pounds, and promptly tripped. I describe myself to this day as looking like Bambi on ice, all arms, and legs everywhere, my Trapper keeper flying with papers everywhere. From that moment on, I was known as Spaz.

Not a great way to start. Even though there were only around 30 students in my grade, it was hard making friends. These kids had grown up together, and I was the new girl. I was used to having at least three cousins and my childhood friends in my classes. How to fit in? I had no idea! No one would sit with me on the 45-minute bus ride to and from school. But very quickly, I started getting the attention of my teachers. Yes, one reason is that I was always talking and trying to be funny, but the main reason was that I was getting good grades and was a bit ahead of the learning curve. Catholic school did pay off for me! In high school, I quickly enrolled in physics, chemistry, and other advanced classes, and started volleyball, basketball, and fast-pitch softball.

I had gained a few close acquaintances but always kept

them at arm's length due to my living circumstances. I was so embarrassed that when I got off the bus, instead of going into the cabin, I would promptly head right to my Grandmother's front door and walk in. I hoped people would think I lived there and not in the little shanty behind her house. While I excelled at sports and academics, I was failing miserably internally: being traumatized by my living conditions had caused me to lie to everyone about everything, act like someone I wasn't, steal to be cool, drink to forget, act promiscuously to be liked, and in general, just not being my authentic self. I was anxious, quick to anger, and a rebel. Lucky for me, things always seemed to go my way, and there were no lasting repercussions for my behavior or actions.
—*Excerpted from Women Who Empower, 2020.*

I have to explain something. In South Milwaukee, my mom always worked, first at the Milwaukee Journal and then as an LPN and visiting nurse. My father was always home to greet me for lunch as I walked home from school and many times afterward as well. He worked at State Sand and Gravel driving a cement truck. Sometimes, I would get to ride in the truck, and many times I got to put my handprint or initials in the wet, cold concrete he had just poured. It was explained to me that my father's refusal to rejoin the Teamsters led to his dismissal (letting his payment membership lapse). But my older cousins alluded to the fact that my father ran numbers and was a bookie. I do remember my dad speaking on the phone and doodling numbers and making them into faces with hats and cigars. One even had a nose like Bob Hope. As I type this, I wish I had thought to save that paper, a little memory of my father, just to have. Needless to say, the bookie angle fits as we did seem to have more money than a secretary or concrete paver would make during that time. Just recently, going back home to Wisconsin to celebrate Thanksgiving with my three brothers, we were talking about our dad. My youngest brother Mike told me something shocking. He told me that our dad once told him a story about how he knew where Jimmy Hoffa was buried: the old Milwaukee County Stadium (Miller Park, now renamed American Family Field).[2] Apparently, when he was pouring concrete and working for the Teamsters, State Sand and Gravel had a contract around that time (1975) at the Stadium. I have never heard my dad lie, nor was he known to have any type of dementia. Again, I wish I could go back in time and ask him more about his job; I guess it will remain a mystery. I always wondered why we moved so far away to our cabin and didn't stay around our family and the only life my father ever knew.

At first, my time at the cabin was adventurous. I had such great, loving, fun memories of visiting my maternal Grandparents every summer. The 8-hour ride I truly looked forward to because halfway there, we would stop in Eau Claire to get McDonald's-such a treat. I would always order my cheeseburger without pickles and mustard, but my dad would often just order, and I would have to wipe it off and throw the pickle away. To this day, while I don't eat red meat, I can't stomach the taste or smell of either pickles or mustard. I remember having several dogs, a mean goat that wouldn't let us up the stairs to enter the cabin, and a rabbit that I think was killed to eat. Maybe this, and the fact that my father hunted and cooked everything he could. There was often "mystery" meat cooking, and I loathed the smell, which contributed to the fact that I no longer eat meat.

During those formative years, nature became my friend. The virgin pine trees, the hay in the fields, picking raspberries on the rock pile (but learning to be afraid of snakes), running in the grass full of bumblebees feasting on the white clover, seeing the gorgeous and colorful northern lights, hearing the wolves on the hill howl at the moon, realizing that I LOVE storms, the thunder and lightning (perhaps because I am a loud storm of electric energy), and most of all the sound and smell of rain. I was making friends with water bugs on a soft

---

2. https://en.wikipedia.org/wiki/American_Family_Field

oasis of mossy rocks, brushing my teeth in the trout stream as a special treat, walking the deer trails with my dad, and being the driver or noise maker while donning bright orange. During the heat of the summer, we would take a ride down to the Gordon Flowage and sometimes bring an old tractor inner tube to float on. Whoever wasn't on it at the time would swim up under it to tip the person on it over. I was always getting scratches from the airflow value because the cap was lost, huge welts on the back of my thighs, and to this day, I have a small scar on my right knee that should have required stitches. In so many ways, I loved being up North, but I was starting to become separate from my true Spirit. A piece of Soul was stolen. The ego was emerging, and I was becoming disconnected, minute by minute, day by day, year by year, from Soul; but I wouldn't see this until almost 40 years later.

So this unscarred, naive childhood ended when I was around 13, and the shame would remain for decades afterward. Shame can cause all types of problems: anxiety, acting out, and losing of Oneself. My shame was a direct result of holding onto the secret of reality and poverty I was living in. When we moved to this tiny cabin, my parents had put our belongings, most of our furniture, all of our family pictures (albums and albums of them), and clothes in my Aunt and Uncle's basement until we could retrieve them. This was the first lesson for me on non-attachment to things. Shortly after we moved up North, we found out that there was a flood and that absolutely everything was damaged. We promptly drove back down to South Milwaukee and tried to salvage anything we could, but it was too far gone. I remember there was one soggy box that we brought back home, but it soon molded, and we threw that away as well. That's what I regret most about this trauma. My brothers and I have no pictures to remember our childhood and family experiences. Occasionally, a cousin will text message me an old picture of me, but that is it.

I remember the first time I got drunk was in the 8th grade. My family visited friends from South Milwaukee the first year after moving to the Northwoods. I was right back with my old friends and at my girlfriend Julie's boyfriend's house above some bar. Who knows where his parents were. We were drinking and everyone had a curfew except me. I might have, but I was not going to adhere to it. After everyone left, I made out with Julie's boyfriend (Igor, Ivan?) and walked home. I woke up to a loud knocking. It was Julie at my parent's friend's house first thing in the morning. Imagine how upset she was when I came to the door with hickeys all over my neck. Hey, I was the cool out-of-town girl, wise beyond her years, and I felt powerful above her. I distinctly remember telling Julie the day or two before that I had already lost my virginity, which was a complete lie, but once again garnered myself attention. I have not spoken to Julie since. She was the same Julie that I met on the first day of Kindergarten. This was the first time I sabotaged a friendship, but sadly not the last time. This was also the first time that I realized I had power sexually over men and that it would allow me to fit in.

The first time I felt peer pressured and less valued outside of my family to act a certain way, to be a certain way, without a doubt, would be during these times in middle school and high school in Minong, WI. Before living in South Milwaukee, I was considered a ringleader: telling others what to do, controlling them, and molding them to my desires. But once the ego of fitting in hit, it was game over. My wild and innate nature was tamed, subdued, and locked away, lest being shamed or ridiculed for my uniqueness or thoughts. I also was a bookworm yet loud, organized yet clumsy, casual friends with everybody, and very prone to drama or performing for attention.

I want to talk about my body and appearance. I was 5' 9 ½ with size 9 ½ (more like 10) size shoes. I had dirty blonde feathered hair, a small frame, buck teeth, with one of my front ones protruding crookedly, and a prominent nose. Back then, I weighed all of 120 pounds, with no curves whatsoever. I tended to be amenorrheic due to my high metabolism and the fact that I played sports throughout the year. Junior year,

I got my first overly large pair of glasses for nearsightedness that I hid behind. It wasn't my best look for years. I was once a cute soft baby duck that had suddenly turned into the teenage "ugly duckling." That all changed as I got off the school bus on the first day of senior year, and a friend of mine, Bill F. started shouting down the hallway, "Bobby's got boobs!" I was getting noticed at the point in my life when my appearance would become important to me. It allowed me to feel special and accepted and gave me self-worth. Around this time was my first experience with bulimia. My friend S.A. told me she was doing it, throwing up after eating, and I idolized her. I remember going home, eating an entire box of mac and cheese and promptly running to the outhouse to throw it up. The feelings of euphoria! While I did not continue this practice regularly, I used it as a form of self-medication every time that I felt bad about something. It continued off and on into my 40s during periods of despair.

    I never felt that I matched my family genetically. As a matter of fact, I would introduce my dad as my dad, and my mom as his wife. I have never seen a picture of my mom pregnant, and I always wondered and had the feeling that I was adopted. I really don't resemble anyone in my family . . . it was just a feeling I had. Also, I have a much different personality. Even to this day, I am so ambitious, outgoing, and fearless that I have to question where that came from. I always wanted my Auntie Irene to be my mom. I even asked her if I could move in with her when I was stuck in poverty. I also always appeared to upset my father or tip over the apple cart. He was always agitated at me, probably because I was always challenging him. There were many holiday dinners that were ruined. Imagine having a quiet mother and a father who just wanted peace and quiet, and then me coming along; a wild child disrupting the calmness and continuity of life. True Soul has always run its own race, never really believing or feeling that I fit in anywhere. Instinctively, I have always known that I have this wild side, and that no matter what, I need to be strong and continue on the path to greater things. I knew that someday I would either be famous, do great things, gain huge recognition, or put my mark on this world in an incredible way. I have always continued to live life intensely, sometimes with silent determination, but most often forcefully. But over time, I learned to walk on eggshells so as not to upset the status quo or stun them (parents, friends, significant others, coworkers, etc.) with my frenetic energy. I could pick up on changes in energies, reading people's faces, and because of that, I learned to succeed on my own by trying to fit in.

Drinking was a common theme during high school and college, and I am sad to say it has continued with me for most of my life. After being cast as one of the leads in *The Egg and I* as a freshman, of course, there was an after-party. I recall drinking sloe gin fizzes, a red syrupy pine-needle tasting drink. In no time at all, I was a slobbering mess. Two upperclassmen boys decided to pick me up and throw me out into a snowbank to sober me up. I don't remember much after that. It was my first time being blacked out, but I have glimpses of throwing up red on my cream cable knit sweater, being driven home, and waking up with my head and mouth hurting, with wood particles in my mouth. I must have hit a branch or a stump when I landed in the snow. Only through the grace of Universal Source was I not taken advantage of or did not die that night.

Like most teenagers, I remember being picked on. Either because of the way I was such a klutz, or my zaniness, or my constant need for attention. There are two occasions involving a lot of alcohol that I want to share. I was at a party with most of my small class. I can't remember what I was drinking, but I know I had a lot of it-drunk. We were all outside and I found myself alone. I decided to bite myself on the arm. Yes, you read that correctly. I decided to bite myself on the arm. I then told all my classmates that a woodchuck had bitten me! Well, as you can imagine, the parents of my friends could tell exactly that it was a human bite, and one of the girls started laughing and started calling me "Chuck." I was so humiliated. This girl would ride the bus with me, laugh, and call me that name for the next year, getting others to call me that as well. I was tormented and ashamed. Exiled from this group, and I never really felt fully back into the circle. This did not help me with my immense complex of the shame of living in poverty and wanting to fit in. The cruelness, the obliviousness to my pain would allow me to believe that I was not good enough, and this negative thought process became detrimental to Soul. I believed that I could not reverse it and that no matter who I was, I would never again be accepted by anyone. I could no longer be my authentic Spirit, and I believe this was the tipping point of no return to me. I would start the decades-long façade of lying, not only to others but to myself as well, to become someone else.

I can only remember listening to and feeling pressured by my dad to change one time in my life. That's the truth! It was when I started wearing a watch that I received as a gift from my Grandma R. It *felt right* to wear it on my right wrist. After a few days, my father noticed it and told me it should be worn on the left. His exact words were, "Don't be ridiculous. Everyone knows you wear a watch on the left side." I promptly changed it over to the correct wrist. Even as I type this, I realize that I should have never listened to him. He never wore a watch a day in his life so what would he know about it? My father had expectations about how I should act. That I should be like everyone else, and this just fit into my earlier beliefs with my friends, don't rock the boat or be yourself, learn to fit in, conform, and be that perfect daughter. I tried. But, now and again, that wild child would come out. I would stay overnight at someone's house after a party and not call my parents. They would have to call the school in the morning to make sure I was there. In other instances, on weekends, I would spend time together with older groups of 19 to 21-year-olds, drinking and acting cool. When it was time to go home, one of the guys offered to give me a ride home, and of course, we made out before I got out of the car. My father threw a conniption fit at 2:30 a.m. when he saw who I was with. That guy happened to be married, but I had no idea. I always tested the limits and boundaries, breaking them, and setting my own rules. I was never submissive to my father, ever. But to his credit, he knew I was a tough one and that I could figure things out on my own. This is a downfall of mine, never asking for help or receiving from others.

Soul shined and came out whenever I felt safe and accepted. Once when I was at a pompom squad camp, around a different group of friends who I probably would never see again. I was feeling so happy and authentic, dancing freely and expressing myself. I looked at a girl and literally thought that she had a bunch of bananas on her head. I asked her, "Why do you have bananas on your head?" She looked at me like I was crazy and said, "It's not bananas, it's a yellow bow!" Now it might be the fact that I had not yet realized that I needed glasses for nearsightedness, but I like to think that I was in my playful, childlike joy, which is what my heart went to. At that camp, when it was time for the awards ceremony, of course I won the "Wild and Crazy Girl Award." I still exhibit this type of behavior today. For the life of me, I can't remember names or faces! Often I will yell at people at a distance and call them by another name. Most of the time, they just smile and say, "You must be mistaken." Just note that I now wear contacts for nearsightedness, and didn't back then, so it's either that I couldn't see, or it was my weird sense of humor Spirit glistening through.

I wanted to feel safe and secure. I knew that I didn't feel that from my living conditions, my parents, or my current group of classmates. So I did what every adolescent did and turned to other friends. Attention gave me power, a feeling of being normal when really what I was feeling inside was a void: not being good enough, not being cared for, not feeling safe, not having enough to eat, not having a place to sleep, and not having clothes to wear. I was coming from a place of lack rather than being grateful for the abundance I did have. Overall, I feared not being cared for financially. When would the other shoe drop? When would I lose it all again?

I was always challenging and inquisitive. I always asked

questions- standing up to authority, being a right fighter, challenging the current existing state of things. This would get me in trouble later on in my adult life. So many whys and hows? I am sure I drove people, especially teachers, crazy. I questioned and wanted to find out the truth in all circumstances. If it didn't feel right to me and ultimately Soul, I would push back and argue, being true and authentic to what felt right for me at the time. Curiosity killed the cat, the old adage goes, but in this case other humans killed my questions and chipped away at Spirit. Disobeying orders and directives, along with not believing things as universal law, had always been my normal.

    I never really fit in with any one group. I was always flitting from one group to the next: whether that be the advanced science student group, the athletes, or even the burnouts as we called them back in the day. I was always struggling to fit in somewhere. But I was lucky. I was a chameleon and belonged to each of these groups in Spirit. But what I really needed at that time was a group that was "fairy-ish." My made-up word. I needed people who loved being outdoors but were magical, light, and deep thought-provoking people, helping me realize that crystals, sage, and tinctures could clear energy and invigorate Spirit. But because it took me 55 years before I found that group, I always felt like an outcast.

    Some of the ways that teenagers try to fit in can consist of stealing, acting promiscuously, drinking, doing drugs, and just all around acting out. I was no exception to this rule, and I did all of these things. The first time I stole something in order to fit in was at one of the only stores in town. This store was not only a grocery store on one side and had a clothing and shoe store on the other side. I heard about how to steal from a few females in my class, going up to the city of Superior, heading into a mall there trying on clothes, and either wearing them out of the store or throwing them in their bags. This was in the early 80s, so obviously, before the clothes had security tags on them. I was intrigued. After all, this would help me not look poor if I had the latest fashions to wear to school! I walked into the store with a friend of mine, C.C., and we both tried on a pair of shoes that fit us and left our old ones in the new box and walked out the door. It was so easy that I couldn't wait to do it again. The next time I was with A.B. who was actually there to try on and purchase bib corduroy overalls, which were all the rage back then. I found a pair, and without trying them on, I stuffed them into my jacket and hissed under my breath to her, "Hurry up!" She thought I was mad at her, and she scurried to follow me out. When we were around a block away, I finally pulled out my much too-large green corduroy bib overalls, and she was mortified at me. Obviously, she did not steal and was judging me for doing so. I only stole one more time in college, from a big chain store, double layering polo shirts with the collars popped, which was also in fashion at the time. But 50 years later, I can still remember the look of disgust and dismay on A.B.'s face. For me, the thrill and adrenaline rush wasn't there after the first couple of times, so I stopped.

My school chose to hold a Junior Prom with Court versus a Senior Prom. As most of us can recall, being nominated to be on the court was a popularity contest. As we sat in a classroom and wrote down our six female and six male choices for Court, I was feeling confident. I had a good gut feeling about being on Court as there were 29 boys and only 12 girls in my class! The boys' names were called first; no surprises there. Then the girls' names: A.B., J.M., H.C., M.M., E.M., and C.M. I was devastated and embarrassed. How could this have happened? I had so many friends in so many diverse groups of people! I think a week or so must have gone by, and I was over it when a rumor started going around about C.M. being pregnant. Pregnant! Well, that would change things. How dare they allow a pregnant female to represent the popular vote, especially as her boyfriend was a freshman! So a few of us started shunning her, being mean girls, and eventually made her feel so shameful that she dropped out of the running for Prom queen.

Dear C.M.,

I want to tell you that I am so deeply sorry for my part in your being ostracized for getting pregnant. You were so young, and mistakes happen. I'm sorry. I love you. Please forgive me.

—B.

With C.M. dropping out, it meant that there was an uneven number, so once again, we would have to choose a single female to take her place. And that person would be . . . me. I was chosen by default and higher than ever odds. I was thrilled. Did I mention that somehow, come hell or high water, I always get my way and things manage to always work out in my favor? The drama didn't end there, however, a few days later C.M. found her strength and decided she *did* want to be on Prom court and took her personal power back. This meant that we now had to choose an additional boy to even things out and re-vote for King and Queen. I will share the outcome of this story later in a sequential order of events.

In another attempt at an effort to fit in, I listened most closely to one of my close friends, S.A. Her family had a lot of money for living in northern Wisconsin. She came to the area when her dad's work transplanted them. She always had the best clothes, and when she turned 16, she got a brand-new Mazda RX7. Later in my life, I would tell people the story as if I was the one that received this car for my birthday. I idolized her and wanted to be her. She had the life I envied. I was invited over to her house to get dressed and picked up for Prom. I had borrowed (from someone in Superior, who to this day I don't remember) a long white prairie buttoned-in-the bust Prom dress with teeny, little flowers on it, with shoulder straps that tied and bought a cropped white coat to wear with it. While we were doing our makeup S. said to me, "Bert, you should wear your hair up this way for Prom." I knew deep down that I did not want to wear it up. I did not like it; it wasn't me. Her mom agreed, telling me that it would be so pretty to put some baby's breath in the back. So I agreed. I felt like such an imposter. It was so unnatural and nothing like me. Years later, I realized that this was just one of many times that I had given my personal power away by not speaking up.

J.N. picked me up, we took pictures, and we went to a small restaurant to eat. I was a bit nervous. When J. ordered his meal, Prime Rib if I recall, I ordered a glass of milk! So funny. I don't know if I just wasn't hungry or I couldn't find anything on the menu I liked, but I do remember him being offended. At Prom, we walked up to the stage, and the winner of King was announced; it was my date J.N.! I was so proud of being on his arm. Next up was Queen, and as karma is always a b*%ch, it was C.M., the pregnant girl!

Up until this time, my promiscuity consisted of playing spin the bottle and making out with guys. Once in 8th grade after a dance party, I went into the closet for 7 Minutes in Heaven with F.H., who I considered my first boyfriend. Ironically, in the present day, he now identifies as gay. Was it something I did? Ha! I digress. My first real sexual experience was the junior night after Prom; typical right? I was at an afterparty, drinking a lot on an empty stomach, passing out on the couch, then coming to, kissing my Prom date, and being dragged into a spare bedroom. I remember passing out again and waking up to my date on top of me, and because I was a virgin, telling him ouch. He could not get past my hymen, and after several tries, he just gave up. I want to preface that I fully intended to lose my virginity that night, and while I was incapacitated and drunk, it was, for all intents and purposes, consensual. The next day I remember being embarrassed that he couldn't enter me fully. So I took a mirror down there and saw that my hymen was torn halfway. I took my nails and broke the rest of it open myself. I would never have this shame again. Stereotypically, my date never spoke about it to me, and we never dated again. From that point on, I learned that sex was power. I felt I could be liked and keep a man if I did what he wanted, so I would have sex with them. There were a few other drunken sexual encounters in high school until I started dating my longer-term boyfriend senior year.

While I did hang out and was friendly with the burnout group, I never smoked or tried marijuana until later in the summer of my junior year. I was at the usual weekend party with upperclassmen and others who had already graduated. We had a keg full of beer and various mixed drinks (which I preferred), and I could smell marijuana throughout the house. This household was well known as the "pot" house, with both the parents and the kids imbibing. My father was friends with both the dad and the mom, sitting with them at the local bars, and liked them quite a bit. Around midnight or 1:00 a.m., my father was supposed to come pick me up. He pulled up, and I remember everyone saying, "Hide the beer and liquor. Mr. C. is coming!" My dad walked in and said, "Hey, isn't anyone going to offer me a beer?" My dad, at 6' 5 inches tall, with size 13 shoes, a big bushy beard, deep voice, most people were very afraid of him. He often wore suspenders over his plaid hunting shirt and always either black pants or blue jeans to try to cover his large testicular hernia. There was a collective sigh of relief. Someone handed him a beer. He took a couple of swigs and promptly asked, "Who's got the wacky tobacky?" I about died. Once again, someone offered him the joint, and he took a hit off it and looked at me and said, "I want to see what the big deal is all about. If you are going to try it, you might as well do it in front of me," passing me the blunt. I took a puff and started coughing, not being able to hold it in. I took a second small inhale. I think my dad finished a beer or two, I finished my red Solo cup drink, and we proceeded to drive the six miles home. When we got there, I started to go to bed and my father started eating chips and dry roasted peanuts, his favorite. A little while later he exclaimed, "I don't know what the big deal all it did was make me hungry." That was the last time I smoked marijuana until I was in my mid-40s.

 Trying to be someone I was not was exhausting. For years, like many women, I am sure I was always apologizing. Always trying to fix what was wrong with me. Seeking counseling, giving up drinking, and thinking I had a psychosis. As Clarissa Pinkett Estes says in one of my favorite books, *Women Who Run with the Wolves*, it was like I was a swan trying to fit in with bears, snakes, slugs, and foxes. I wanted to swim, but they expected me to run or crawl. Shape shifting into whatever group or person I was close to at the time. But what I didn't realize was that I wasn't even a swan. I was a Starseed (as defined earlier) whose mission is to bring Light and knowledge, but I wouldn't realize this for several years to come.

Senior year awards ceremony: I sold the first painting I ever painted. Although proud of the money I got for my purple mountain scene at the time, I now wonder if the buyer was taking pity on the girl living in poverty and just letting her save face by handing her $25. But I also lettered in several sports, including football, as I was one of the statisticians, and I heard my name being announced for a small scholarship to go to college. Then, another accolade with award money. Finally, the big one of the evening- Outstanding Senior in Science, goes to . . . me. Wow. I beat out each one of the 41 students graduating with me. Writing this sentence, you can tell that I was extremely competitive at the time. It's all I had. "If it is meant to be, it's up to me," became my internal motto without me knowing it. At the time, I knew I would do anything I had to do to get out of my current situation, go to college, and never move back to those conditions again. Education would become my way out, and I would never look back.

With my scholarship money and the help of Pell Grants and student loans, I started at the University of Wisconsin, Barron County, in the Fall of 1983. I was still acting like a wild child, and after almost flunking out at the end of my first year, I decided to do something drastic because everyone told me I wouldn't cut it: join the Army Reserves. I signed on for six years. While I never took advantage of the GI bill, I continued going to school and taking out student loans.

—Excerpted from Women Who Empower, 2020

PART II:
Adulthood and Ego

The Winter: Shattered Fragments

> "On the inside, I was fearful, untrustworthy, anxious, felt guilty, and had low self-esteem. I find this still to be true even as I type this sentence in my 50-year-old adult life."
>
> —*Me*

I think I really started to push myself, my agenda and what my ego wanted, right before my first year in college. My first long-term boyfriend, J.K. was also my high school boyfriend who gave me a small diamond promise ring for a graduation present. I remember my female classmates coming up to gaze upon it, and I was a bit annoyed that everyone was making such a fuss over a chip of a diamond. J. ended up following me to UW Barron County for our freshman year of college.

During this time, I met a female friend S. who lived off campus. She was fun-loving, pretty, dressed well, and drove a black Trans Am. I remember she wore a lot of makeup compared to me and always smelled good. I was infatuated with her, not in a sexual way, but in a way that I wanted to be her. As we became better friends, I found out that she was in the military, the Army Reserves.

In September of our freshman year, Randy Clark, two years older than me in high school, who I had casually dated a few times, was one of the first Marines to get killed in Lebanon in 1983. Randy joined the Marines right after high school to take advantage of better schooling, and right before he was deployed to Beirut, he expressed anxiousness about being stationed over there. His sister, who was a good friend of mine, gave me the news that he had passed. I promptly went home to pay my respects, but somewhere in the mix-up of the press and the news coverage was given the wrong time that the funeral would be held. I never had a chance to properly grieve or say goodbye to him. I mention this story because somewhere, I got it in my mind that I too would join the military, and that I would do it for Randy and to prove to others that I was not just a *Private Benjamin*-type girl.

S. helped me find a recruiting station, and on March 15th, 1984, I promptly signed up for the Army Reserves, knowing I wanted to go into Intelligence, on a whim, telling no one until after I had crossed my t's and dotted my i's on my enlistment papers. I would finish out my first year of college, and in the summer of 1984, then I would report to Fort Dix, NJ for basic training. I don't really think my dad was too upset with me. He probably thought it was for the best to try to straighten me out some. But I believe after I told him what I did, he said something like, "What? Why the hell did you do that?"

During freshman year, I lived with three strangers in a two-bedroom, co-ed apartment on campus. When I went to college, I did not yet have my license, but I was working hard to obtain it. The girl that I had to share my side of the bedroom with was a mousy, awkward, dare I say, weird girl. She did not drink, party, or have a boyfriend. My other two roommates were most similar to me. However, I distinctly remember one of them cooking bear stew one weekend and being physically repulsed by the smell of it. One weekend, when my bedroom mate went home, I decided to snoop through her belongings and her locker chest. What I found in there freaked me out. I found some candles, some weird books, and most alarming to me at the time was a scarf with a pentagram on it! OMG, I thought, she is a freaking witch. I could not deal with that. Black magic and spells being cast about. So I did a terrible thing. I went to the boys and my boyfriend's apartment across the hall and stole a clock radio.

I put it in her trunk, and when B.F. realized it was missing, we searched all around, and I found it among her stuff. We accused her (I just realized the similarities to the Salem witch hunts and the judgment associated there). She was so upset that she ended up leaving the dorm rooms, and I got a new roommate the next semester.

At the end of our first semester I had won a beer-drinking contest that made the school newspaper, barely passed classes of English, remedial algebra, chemistry, and physics, and my boyfriend realized that college wasn't for him. He decided to move out to Oregon and work in a lumberyard that his brother-in-law owned. During the semester break, we drove cross country with my own cedar chest full of my personal belongings, as I was going to meet him after freshman year and transfer to another University out there.

The second semester, I took the same exact classes, but they ended with II. The partying continued, but something new took over, my promiscuity. That ultimately resulted in me cheating on my boyfriend with everyone from a male that lived next door, to a few one-night stands. During this semester, I put a tremendous amount of pressure on my boyfriend to buy me things, send me cards, flowers, and call me constantly. I soon found out that I could wrap another male around my little finger, other than my dad, by getting him to buy me the finer things in life. I think this was my first realization that I could mold men into something so perfect for me, to fit into my love story that I made up in my mind that I honestly believed at the time that he could be the one I would spend my life with.

When my boyfriend would call me and I could not be reached, I think he finally got the picture of what I was doing. It was soon after that I heard he started dating a girl that worked at the Hallmark store where he used to buy me cards. I believe he is still with her 40 years later!

The partying caught up to me, and by the spring, I was flunking the majority of my classes. I knew that I had the military to fall back on, and it couldn't have come at a better time. I packed up my limited belongings and boarded my first plane as an adult, excited for the adventure to begin.

Basic Training and Military

> "E-1-3, that's what I want to be. We're rough, we're tough, we cut no slack. You mess with us; we'll break your back. Yayyyyy Echo!"
>
> —*Military cadence song*

Perhaps, I consciously blocked out the memory of arriving at boot camp, or maybe it is just the length of time that has passed. I am thankful for the United States Army Training Center Basic Training yearbook that I came home with to help me write this next section. Unlike the previous and the following sections, which are filled with a lot of angst and strife, I really enjoyed and had a fun time during my time at basic.

As you can guess by now, I was fearless. Nothing could stop me, and if something or someone tried to get in my way, I would viciously fight for what I wanted. It was this tough girl persona that I took on when I first showed up with other females at the reception intake station. As soon as I arrived on May 28th, 1984, along with the other enlisted females, there were long lines that we queued up in. There were rumblings and looks as we were the 1st full female Company to arrive and eventually graduate at Fort Dix and that the news outlets would be around to commemorate the event.

At reception, I undertook more aptitude tests, another physical examination including massive amounts of new vaccinations, a classification interview, general orientation meetings, clothing issue, including being assigned our M16 rifle, and the creation of our permanent file as a soldier in training for the US military. I was no longer a civilian, and the quickness in which this occurred made my head spin. I received my identification necklace, or dog tags, and was told that they had to stay on my person at ALL times. They consisted of a long necklace with my name, social security number, blood type, and religious affiliation, as well as a much shorter loop attached to the longer necklace with a second tag, which was called a toe tag. I will let you imagine what that was used for. I was assigned the MOS or military occupational specialty of a 71L, which is administrative: performing clerical and typing duties until I could pass my language test to become a linguist, and to undergo and meet the requirements of all of my Intelligence Unit security clearances.

The clothing issue was a problem for me. The fit for my Battle Dress Uniform, camouflage pants, or BDUs was a challenge; I have a 36" inseam but at that time only a 26" waist. I had to go up several waist sizes to fit my length and always rolled my pants at the waist, which was inconvenient, to say the least. The most problematic though, was my shoe size. As mentioned earlier, I have a long narrow foot, a size 9 ½, and the Army-issued combat boots were one size, so I sized up to a size 10. Even with double socks on, my heels still slipped in them, and this caused a major issue when marching. But more about that later.

I was assigned a room in the female-only barracks, with a metal framed bunk bed (top) with nine other females, handed a pillow, a set of sheets, and a scratchy wool blanket. There was a footlocker at the end of my bed that I could lock, with a duffle bag for our civilian clothes. We also received an assigned metal locker where we kept our BDUs, toiletries, and rucksack, which had to be neat and tidy at all times in case of a surprise inspection. I had to learn to make my bed with tight 45-degree or hospital corners, so tight that you could bounce a quarter off them. If my sheets were messy, and even if they weren't, there would be many a time after a late night of marching that our room would find our beds overturned and sheets half stripped off, lockers rummaged through for contraband, so that we would have to make them again and tidy up before we went to sleep that night. Bunk and room inspection could come at any time, day or night, and I always had to be tidy. Uniform inspections were routinely done as well. So often during our free time, we would spit-shine our boots to be prepared. If I wasn't ready or my area did not pass inspection, the entire room would suffer the consequences, most likely in the form of push-ups or getting dressed for PT, physical training, and sometimes running for *miles*. This was especially difficult if this happened late at night because our wake-up call was at 5:00 a.m. every morning, sometimes earlier if a Drill Sergeant came in first yelling. Breakfast was around 6:00 a.m. (0600 military time), and "Reveille" was promptly at 7:00 a.m., signaling us to fall into formation for the raising of the flag and roll call. "Taps" being played at 9:00 p.m. (2100 military time) meant that I had seconds to get into bed, and all lights shut off. No talking, or at least not being caught talking, was not permitted after the lights went out.

The mess hall reminded me of an adult version of a high school cafeteria: brown meats with gravy, rice or potatoes, white bread and butter, and some overcooked mushy vegetables every meal. Needless to say, I wasn't impressed and tended to carb-load on bread and starches for most meals. We did share the mess hall with "Joes" or male trainees, and once during my first week, I was passed a note from one of them telling me I was pretty! I fondly, yes fondly, remember KP or kitchen patrol duty, which every trainee was assigned to on a rotational basis. I would have to sit and peel potatoes for what seemed like hours for the entire 1st Battalion (~1000 males and females), but it was most likely just for our Company E (185 females). Company E was further divided into Platoons. I was in the 4th Platoon of approximately 30 women, soon to be my nearest and dearest friends. To this day, I am one of the fastest potato peelers around!

Day-to-day life in basic started officially on June 4th, 1984, and included sitting through boring classes such as first aid, where I learned to apply tourniquets (for obvious reasons) and became experts in bandaging and splinting, evacuation, and treating for shock, bleeding, fractures, snake, spider, or insect bites. There were classes on disassembling, cleaning, and reassembling your rifle, along with timed testing on how quickly we could do this. I never believed or had any thought as to what these classes meant or if I would put them into practice. I knew that, based on my MOS, I would probably never see or experience combat. So for me, they were just another way to quickly pass the eight weeks. The only time I wasn't in classes or training was on Sunday mornings when I could attend Mass and believe me; everyone took advantage of getting out of the barracks and seeing the Joes!

I also sat through core classes for soldiers in principles to live by while protecting themselves and other soldiers on missions, learned verbatim to recite the Soldiers Creed, memorized ranks and grades of Officers, practiced military courtesies as when and who to salute, and numerous other military strategies such as map and compass navigations, and falling quickly into formations (groups) and ranks (lines). Communication courses included learning how to operate radios, satellite phones, all boring stuff! I briefly remember learning how to apply fixes to these methods of COMMS by taking apart and tinkering with the devices. The above classes took around one week to complete, and when I was through with that, the next phase of basic would begin.

Phase two training would last another two weeks and would focus on motivation, teamwork, and the dreaded discipline everyone hears so much about. Immediately after arriving in the first days, physical drill training started. I would march in cadence (call and response), echoing back the verses of my Platoon leader's or Sergeant's songs, doing push-ups or crab walking in full gear. If I got out of sync or if someone was late to formation, the real discipline began. Both of my drill sergeants were male. Sergeant T. was extremely intimidating looking, while Sergeant L., a kind-faced male, were my two drill SSGs. Male Sergeant M. was the Senior Drill Sergeant of Co. E, but I rarely saw him. But when I did, he did not notice me. To say that I stood out and garnered Sergeants' T. and L.'s attention was an understatement. As a tall smiley, blonde, they were immediately drawn to me, to break Spirit, so to say. It could be over the simplest thing, such as your collar on your BDUs not perfectly at the correct angle or your baseball-like cap not sitting on your head properly. The stereotypical yelling in your face and responding back, "Yes, sir," was a daily, or dare I say, an hourly occurrence when in formation. So many times, I could not wipe the smile off my face, they would mispronounce my last name, yelling, "Chmielecki, drop and give me 50," meaning pushups. At that point, I would have to drop out of formation, go to the side, and start counting out loud until I did my 50 pushups, pick up my weapon and other gear, and run to catch up to the rest of the group. It did not matter if it was raining, in a puddle, or on concrete; I just did it. I can proudly say that Spirit was never broken. I was always happy and looked at it as a challenge. One thing that helped was that I was already in great shape from playing sports in high school, so I was used to the physical exertion on my body. Many, many others did not fare as well, and there were many breakdowns. Others went AWOL (absence without leave) by hiding in the showers or in the barracks, and eventually, these individuals were dishonorably discharged, never to be seen again.

For hours on end, I practiced precision marching, presenting of arms with my rifle, standing at ease, snapping to attention for what seemed like long amounts of time, drills with both my platoon, then eventually with the entire company.

Obedience,
Alertness,
Responsiveness.

While writing this, I can hear the rhythmic beat of the "boots on the ground," the weapons snapping in unison, and the strong, proud, loud voices when singing the first part of the song, which varied all of the time, *"I don't know what*

I've been told . . ." to keep us motivated when marching or running.

The one thing that still stands out in my mind during these marches and runs was that around two weeks into training, I developed such severe large blisters on the back of my heels due to my narrow heel and my combat boots slipping that I had to go to medical. I'm talking about the size of a plum! Medical determined that they would not lance them for fear of infection, so I was permitted to wear flip flops (our shower shoes), in rank, until they went down. True story. Imagine how happy I was for the next three weeks. I still prefer wearing flip-flops to walk in, hike in, and to climb the Great Wall of China in. It doesn't surprise me one bit that I developed my agility in flip flops during this time in basic.

In addition to marching, I also had to overcome both the confidence and obstacle courses. The timed confidence course consisted of logs and platforms high up in the tree line. I had to walk along these narrow logs, up steep ladders to help overcome my fear of heights while precariously balancing with full gear on. I am looking at pictures now, and I am not seeing any harnesses or netting below! At the end of it, I shimmied down a long rope to the ground, and must have passed. Once it was accomplished I never had to do it again. The obstacle course was a different story. These challenges were lower to the ground. There were many of the same components: narrow logs, wide ladders that I was required to weave in and out and under the steps while going backward at times. There were solid wood walls with ropes that I had to walk up and then straddle the top to drop back over and run to the next hurdle. There was a high all-rope net wall that was quite difficult for me to master, but with lots of practice, I finally accomplished that feat. The monkey bars were my favorite because it seemed like it was a game versus a challenging task. This course was also timed, and once I passed, I could move on to the next test.

During this phase, I participated in a one-day, one-night training where I learned to: properly apply camouflage paint to my face, dig a foxhole, secure a perimeter, and took turns standing watch. But it was the preparation for nuclear, biological, and chemical (NBC) attacks while properly securing a protective mask and taking it off in a chamber filled with a controlled amount of nerve gas that was most alarming. In order for me to deal with the uncertainty of war, and what might happen, nothing in the seven weeks of training compared to this harrowing experience. I had to watch some films about the effects of CS (orto-chlorobenzylidene-malononitrile) gas, or tear gas, and train on how to properly fit our protective mask to our face. All of us lined up with our masks on outside the chambers, and once inside the foggy room, I could smell a little bit of the gas. I'm guessing my mask wasn't as tight as it should have been. We were instructed to take it off and state our name, rank, and serial number before we could leave (flee!) the chamber. The tear gas is a strong irritant to the mucous membranes, and many of us started crying, getting runny noses, coughing, gagging, drooling, and a few even throwing up. The treatment to reverse these symptoms is air. Once I was outside, I was supposed to open my eyes, which seemed impossible at the time, and run around flapping my arms to get the gas out of my body and off my skin. Within a few minutes, the CS gas left my system, and I was almost back to 100% except for my runny nose. Everyone had to do this drill two times, with the second time being able to clear their mask and put it back on. I hope to never have to do it again. Ironically, it is these images that are captured in pictures, taking up two pages in our yearbook. Thankfully, I am not featured in any of them.

    Phase three of training was my favorite. In this two-week period, we were finally able to go to the rifle range to practice shooting. I grew up around guns, as my family deer hunted in northern Wisconsin, so I practiced shooting at targets many times in my life. In the rifle field training, we learned rifle safety procedures: how to sight our rifles, practiced loading and unloading our clips, and engaging at targets at a range of 25 meters. As we advanced, we engaged with pop-up targets at longer distances, anywhere from 70-300 meters. If I hit accurately, the pop-up target would collapse down only to have another appear in a different spot. I did this while taking different firing positions, and I always found it to be exciting, but once again, I must reiterate that at 18 years old, I did not know that I was in training for combat per se, but I thought it was more of a competitive game of sport. I did not understand the seriousness of what this training actually was for. At the end of this training, I took a test called the Marksman Qualification Badge, and I did not miss one target, so I qualified for the highest 1ST place honor, the Rifle Expert Badge to wear on my dress uniform, hitting 40 targets (some with my gas mask on, some at night as well).

Just a side note to insert here. I wore contacts, but these contacts did not correct my astigmatism at the time. In the military, you are issued military black framed glasses, or as they are jokingly called, birth control glasses (BCG), because they made you look so ugly when you wore them. Fun fact, I can't wink. I can't keep one eye closed when shooting, and since my contacts did not correct my sight fully out on the range, I had to wear my BCGs. Because I couldn't line up the sights of my rifles with one eye, I had to take a black grease pencil and black out the lens of my non-dominant eye, which happens to be my right eye. Imagine what I looked like, as a right-handed shooter, with BCGs on, with one side blacked out. Pretty (ugly)! Yet, I can't complain, as it did the trick.

During these weeks, land navigation was also practiced. During the basic infiltration course, I crawled under barbed wire fences with our rifle in mud on my elbows and knees, careful to stay low while live rounds were being fired overhead and simulated hand grenades exploded around me. At the end of this phase, I took a 2-day, 2-night training to practice all of these skills while packing everything I needed for this time into my rucksack, including a canteen full of water and all my Meal, Ready to Eat kits, better known as MRE's.

Let me explain the two types of food available when away from Fort Dix. Field chow was hot food, or slop more aptly named, that we received while on overnights. It was served cafeteria style, eaten off paper plates, most often than not: morning, noon, and night, and mostly lukewarm and a runny indistinguishable mess. As you can imagine, this was absolutely disgusting, and I only took what I thought I could stomach. But after long days of miles and miles of marching and intense physical training, most of the time, I was famished. While field chow was lukewarm, MREs were tough to handle because they were cold. We did get a little Sterno burner to heat the meat, but it rarely worked, so it wasn't worth the time to try. They came prepackaged in either tin cans or brown sealed plastic and were high in caloric content, and while presented to us in a cardboard box, we broke them down before to save room and keep some for a snack at a later time. These prepackaged meals usually contained white saltine crackers, liquid cheese spread or peanut butter, some type of brown mystery meat in gravy, which I ALWAYS traded, and a dessert. Beechies chewing gum was always included as well, not for novelty but as a necessity in case a soldier couldn't brush their teeth. I would only eat the crackers, cheese, and peanut butter and stockpile all of the desserts: brownies, cherry nuts, or chocolate nut cakes (my favorite), or cookies to eat later or at a different meal.

During this time in basic, specifically on June 23rd, I turned 19. It was also around this time I was ¾ of the way through training, and for some reason, my platoon was given a pass on a Sunday evening to visit the Pink Flamingo, a club on base that served alcohol and was known as an officer's club. We were allowed to drink, play pool, and dance with "Joes" for a one-night reprieve! This was a rare occurrence for trainees to get to experience, but I have to say it has stuck out in my mind as one of the best birthdays I have ever had. Early formation the next morning was tough but having a few cocktails the night before, it was so worth it.

During the final weeks of basic training, things ramped up. In this last phase, I learned different fire and maneuvering techniques, and engaged targets with a team going through and around abandoned buildings. I sat in classes learning to identify and disable land mines, specifically the AP-51. In the field, I would set up the mine pointing it at the intended target, enable it to make it live, roll the wire and crawl backward away from the device, take cover, and push the button to detonate. I also was trained in advanced weapons: firing M60 machine guns, launching the M72 light anti-tank weapon (LAW), and throwing live hand grenades.

The hand grenade class was the most serious class. Extreme precautions, from learning the types, characteristics, and capabilities, and all of the safety features were drilled into me again and again. Then even before I even set foot on the hand grenade assault course (HGAC), I practiced positions and throwing techniques with dummy or inactive grenades and identifying hand and pyrotechnic signals. Finally, after around a week, I was able to practice throwing live grenades. I played softball in high school, so once again, this was a favorite training of mine. Yet I did not realize or truly comprehend the gravity of the activity. I would lie on the ground in a low trench that I dug, pull the pin, pop up to see the target, which was a foxhole, and have just seconds to launch before it exploded. I would also practice running, falling, pulling, throwing as well. At the end of the training, I took a test for hand grenade throwing at 20-, 25-, and 35-meter foxhole targets, both in the standing and prone positions. I once again scored 1st place, passing all 7/7 stations, once again giving me an Expert Grenade Medal to wear.

The last training before graduation was a 3-day, 3-night bivouac camp, setting up my own tent, eating only MREs, practicing all skills up to this point, digging my own latrine and foxhole with a buddy, marching between 10-15 kilometers to the site dressed in full gear with helmet, rifle, carrying all equipment and food in my rucksack and water in my canteen, complete with camouflage makeup. This assessed my survival, fitness, and soldier skills. Afterward, my final tests were given End of Cycle Test or Soldier Stakes (EOCT)- passing 212 tasks 30/30 points, which were learned to receive

100%, and the Army Physical Fitness Test (APFT)- 100 push-ups, 78 sit-ups, 2 mile run in under 15:36 minutes for an 18-year-old female to score 100%. Since I received 100% in all these tests, along with scoring 1st overall in the Company Drill Competition with my platoon, my last commendation was to be awarded Honor Platoon of Cycle 34–84, E-1-3, 4th platoon.

The time had arrived for me to get fitted for my Army Class A dress uniform: dark green blazer and skirt, light green shirt, black neck tab, black beret, and low black heels to wear at graduation. I officially graduated from basic training Friday, July 27th, 1984. I would later obtain my security clearance as a Reservist, serving at Fort Snell, MN, of the 523rd Army Security Agency (ASA), Military Intelligence Unit, Deployment Support Command (DSC) for the next six years, until my honorable discharge on March 14th, 1990.

First Love and Anxious Attachment

"The magic of first love is our ignorance that it can ever end."

—Benjamin Disraeli

Since I was to be stationed in Minneapolis for my Reserve Unit, I moved there within a few days of returning home from basic and promptly enrolled in Normandale Community College to finish my studies. I was able to move into a house with my mom's good childhood friend and her family to help me get on my feet. I signed up for Nutrition classes, and within two years I received my Associate of Science degree with a concentration in Nutrition. I was so close to receiving my Associate of Arts Degree that I stayed one more year and received that as well. It was during this time that most of my inner trauma: rejection wounds of being less than, or never enough, feelings really started to show.

I found a new group of friends at the college in which to

party and drink with. I stayed out late at night, did not eat, and my weight was still low, somewhere around 125. I even had a professor in one of my Nutrition classes question me if I had an eating disorder. No, I didn't, but I wasn't taking care of myself either. Up until this point, I was just using alcohol until I wasn't. I met D., a guy quite a bit older than me, and started dating him. I was impressed and infatuated with his fancy cars, house, and what I considered a *rich* lifestyle. We had a tumultuous relationship, and it was at a party one night that a friend of his introduced me to cocaine. I tried it and found that I enjoyed the energy it gave me, especially staying up to study. D. was not happy with this friend of his, but somehow from that point on, it was always available to me.

D. was my first "love," and oh boy, did I have grandiose ideas about him and for him. After one year of dating, I told him I was expecting a full-length white fur coat for Christmas with a diamond engagement ring in one pocket and keys to a car in another. No pressure! I must have been very persistent because D. listened to me the best he could, and I received a white, Blue Fox shin-length fur coat, a cubic zirconia ring in one pocket, but the other pocket was empty. Disappointment immediately set in, and I pressured him until I got the ¾ marquis poor quality diamond ring with the yellow gold step band I had been hoping for. The keys to the car would come later when he found me a great deal on a baby blue with a white top SS Monte Carlo with low miles and plastic still on the back seat; however, I paid for it.

I promptly moved in with him, knowing in my heart that he would remain a bachelor for life, and things quickly continued to go downhill. For years I kept pressuring him to buy me things and start planning our wedding, but he kept stalling and pushing back. One evening after a long night of drinking, the anger became explosive on both sides, and the police were called in. At this point, I knew I needed to move out. I enrolled at Saint Catherine's College, an all-women's Catholic college in St. Paul, MN, to finish up my bachelor's degree. I found a job that provided housing, returned the ring, and did not look back.

Modeling and Prince

> *"Let's go crazy*
> *Let's get nuts*
> *Let's look for the purple banana*
> *Until they put us in the truck, let's go"*[1]
>
> —*Song lyrics from Let's Go Crazy*
>
> Written by: Prince Rogers Nelson. Lyrics © Universal Music Publishing Group. Lyrics Licensed & Provided by LyricFind[2]

During this period in my life, I was still partying hard with drugs and alcohol. I am not really sure how I fell into modeling, but I do remember meeting a few models at a club one night. They suggested that I "try-out" by walking for someone at Dayton Hudson for a fall show that was coming up. Now the only thing that I had going for me at the time was that I was tall and thin. I quickly found a photographer to help me with some headshots and had 100 black and whites printed with my name, height, weight, hair and eye color, dress, blouse, slack, and shoe size. This was *be*fore email or cell phones were popular, so if they contacted me, the bookers would call me on my home phone.

I showed up in downtown Minneapolis, Nicollet Mall Street, the headquarters of Dayton Hudson, to "walk." I was dressed in a short-waisted blue blazer with gold buttons, a white shell top, white silk pants, and 2-inch white heels, and my hair pulled back into a tight low bun with minimal makeup on. I was 22 years old. The booker asked me to walk several times back and forth across her office, took my

---

1. Retrieved on December 3rd, 2022, from: https://www.lyrics.com/lyric/114771/Prince/Let%27s+Go+Crazy
2. https://www.lyricfind.com/

number down, and said they would be in touch. A few days later, I received the call that I had booked my first runway show, The 1987 Dayton's Fall Oval Room Show.

A few agencies had seen me walk at that first show, so I made a few rounds and ended up being represented by two agencies in the Twin Cities, Portfolio I Model and Talent Agency and Plaza 3 Talent and Model Agency, which was also a profitable modeling school. Lynn was my booker at Plaza 3, but I can't remember who I worked with at Portfolio I. More runway auditions, along with print, commercial, and movie auditions, were booked. Many of them I got, and some I didn't. The feedback given was either I was "too tall" or "too commercial looking." As a result, my modeling resume had many more runway shows on it than print work.

If I was partying hard before, modeling turned everything up a notch. Taking classes during the day, going home to change and dress up for the next audition across town usually, taking a bump, then heading back home to get re-ready to go hit the clubs, drinking, dancing, and doing more drugs until closing time at 1:00 or 2:00 a.m. After that, I would then head somewhere to an after-party, stumble home to sleep for a few hours, and repeat the cycle.

One day, during an audition, I caught the eye of a male model. We ended up auditioning together for a print opportunity. Although I did not get the booking, K. asked me for my phone number, and we went out. He was the most gorgeous man I had ever laid eyes on and I fell hard and fast for him. After around three months of dating, I pressured him for an engagement ring, which as you can tell by now was a common theme for me. He relented, presenting me with a nearly flawless 1-carat emerald cut diamond flanked by two medium-sized baguettes. Neither of us had even met each other's parents yet! I had been burning the candle at both ends, extremely anxious and not quite yet addicted to substances, but partying nightly and stressed beyond belief. I did not have time for a relationship and would snap at him constantly. He was into cocaine as well. At one after-party, we were both doing drugs in the bathroom of a person neither of us knew, and suddenly, someone started pounding on the door. Two men burst in with handguns, shouting and screaming, looking for someone else. This was somewhat of a wake-up call for me, and we both immediately high-tailed it out of there.

    I would not party with anyone I did not know ever again. I cut down dramatically on the cocaine I took and the amount of alcohol I drank. This was extremely difficult for me because in the 80s, everywhere I turned around someone had drugs to offer. Whether it be my modeling friends, people I didn't know, or a good friend of mine from St. Kate's that would snort coke off the hood of her car before class in the parking lot. It was readily available for free. In my mind, I was proud because I never had to buy anything. I only tried some quaalude pills one time to bring me back down after staying up all night grinding my teeth from cocaine, but other than that, I did not try other drugs offered, such as acid, mushrooms, or black beauties.

    One evening I decided not to go out to the clubs and tried calling K. He wasn't picking up, so I decided to drive over to his house. I walked in and couldn't find him, even though his car was in the driveway. I walked out on the back porch to see if he was in the jacuzzi and found him with another girl half naked. I screamed. Although she left, I fought with him all night and in the wee hours of the morning had sex with him. I woke up feeling like sh*t and started the fight with him all over again. I knew this would never work, so I took off yet another engagement ring and threw it at him. I never saw him again, not even while modeling.

    It was during this time that I first officially saw Prince perform at 1st Avenue. After several times being in the crowd, always with my model posse (some of whom were already familiar to him), they eventually led me to an official meeting and audition for him. Over the next five years, I developed an acquaintanceship with him, which is evidenced by my appearances in several of his M.T.V., VH1, and B.E.T. music videos (1987, 1988, 1990), *Purple Rain* (1987) and ending with *Graffiti Bridge* (1990). I had small speaking roles in both movies, and you can catch glimpses of me in many of his videos and one of his protégé videos *Bang Bang (1989),* by Brown Mark. Morris Day and the Time, which consists of Jimmy Jam, Terry Lewis, Jerome Benton; Sheila E., George Clinton, and Kim Basinger were all seen around the set at one point or another. All of these were filmed at his studio, Paisley Park in Chanhassen, under very secretive conditions. One of us models would receive a call from someone on his team instructing us to be somewhere at some ungodly hour, usually around 4 a.m., to be picked up and transported to Paisley Park. We would then head straight into wardrobe fitting for costume, be given scripts to look over if needed and slam some coffee or Diet Coke before heading into hair and makeup. Our call time was at 7:00 a.m. and a few minutes before we would all rush down the stairs to get to set before Prince showed up. I remember sitting next to him in the makeup chair, making small talk, and then rushing with him down the stairs to make call time, thinking about how small (short) he was, even with high heel boots on! It is really important to note that Prince had ZERO tolerance for drugs and alcohol on set at that time. He was the consummate professional, focused, and determined. I can still see him impishly smile at me when I was playing a bartender, and I clinked the glasses so hard that the director had to yell, "Cut," and we had to start all over again. When he died, I posted a pay stub that I had kept from Graffiti Bridge. It is sad to think that a musical genius transitioned so soon.

If I wasn't attending classes at St. Kate's, I would be taking classes at Plaza 3. I took courses in theater production, wardrobe, makeup techniques, hair, advanced acting (T. V., commercial, movie), public speaking, voice dictation, voice-overs, production and rehearsal, photography poses, pageant judging for the Miss and Mrs. America system, and various dance classes. I went through every class offered to me, approximately 150 hours total, and eventually, Plaza 3 hired me to teach some of these classes for them. Yet another thing to add to my already crazy, busy schedule.

I would continue to work for Dayton's over the next three years and also worked for: Saks 5th Avenue, the Harold WAMSO benefit show, Burberry's, Anne Klein, River West Condos, Barbara Bridals, Miltons, and the Miss America Pageant. I was a personal runway model for Pauline Trigére, Isaac Mizarahi, Mary McFadden, Bill Blass, Victor Costa, and Adolfo. I have informally modeled appearing in trunk shows for: Revillon Furs, Misha, Ellen Tracey, Ralph Lauren, Calvin Klein, Adrienne Vittadini, Albert Nipon, Valentino, Carolina Herrera, Salvatore Ferragamo, David Hayes, Liz Claiborne, Oleg Cassini, A.J. Bari, Julie Durocher, St. John Knits, and Gloria Sachs. I was also a personal hair model for Philip Kingsley and Horst Rechelbacher, founder of Aveda.

During my modeling career, the models who were consistently getting booked for shows and print work formed a modeling guild, which I was a part of. I stepped away from the agencies and modeling in 1990, but during that time, my approximate rates were: $30 per hour for hair and makeup, $40 per hour for fit modeling for the designer, $55–75 per hour for trunk shows or personal designer modeling in store, $60 per hour for dress rehearsal run through, and $120 per hour per actual show.

Transitions and Other Jobs

"You cannot discover new oceans unless you have the courage to lose sight of the shore."

—Andre Gide

It might surprise you at this point to tell you that the first real job I ever had was at around the age of 20 and that I almost got fired from it because I would not do the work but instead insisted on getting a two-week severance to hold me over until I found a new one. This wasn't to say I was lazy; I have a strong work ethic; it is just an example of what I was not passionate about doing. Typing as a receptionist at the front desk of a broker firm was not my calling! ~Excerpted from Women Who Empower, 2020

The family I was living with in the suburbs of Minneapolis, long before I was married, knew I was out all hour's partying (sometimes with their son), so it was strongly suggested to me that I get a job or face finding another place to live. So at 20, I applied as a receptionist for a real estate brokerage firm, Realty Center. I was hired part-time so that I could still go to college, but I had not yet gotten my driver's license and had to take the bus back and forth to work. While it was only around ½ mile away from my house, it still was a pain. While I enjoyed the people at the firm, I soon became bored. One day after around a year of working there, a broker asked me to type up an MLS (multiple listing service) on the typewriter. These were really a pain in the ass to do, so I told him, "I didn't know how to do that." I wanted to get a different job, and a week later, I found myself looking at the want ads in the local newspaper. I started reading an ad that I thought would be perfect until I scanned to the bottom and realized that it was for my position at Realty Center! Monday morning, I marched right into the head of hiring, acted all indignant, and she promptly offered me a two-week severance.

I had my A.S. in Nutrition, so I applied at Martin Luther Manor (MLM), a senior and transitional living center, and was hired part-time as a Registered Dietetic Technician. This was a bit further from my house, so I ended up getting a 10-speed bike as a gift for my birthday and rode that to and from work. I loved it! It kept me fit and slim and gave me down time to process and relax. But winter was soon coming, and I knew I had to get my license.

I had flunked one driver's road test because when the instructor asked me to turn right, he meant at the stoplight, and I took it to immediately turn right into someone's job. I am sure there were other things I lost points on, but me being spacy regarding instructions did not help matters! I still had a carbon copy of my Wisconsin permit that was soon expiring. I looked at it and noticed that in the box that noted what type of license it was, it had a "P" in it for permit. I asked a friend of mine in class, who recently obtained their Minnesota regular license to see their temporary copy and in the box for what kind of license they had said "PL" for permanent license. Well, you can guess where this is going. I found some carbon copy paper, lined it up, and added an "L" after mine. In order to transfer from a WI to a MN license, all I needed to do was study for a written test. I did not have to take a road test, so I went to the DMV (department of motor vehicles) and passed my test and was sent home with an official license for MN.

But I digress once again. Working at MLM paid well, gave me benefits, and the hours 3–8 p.m. fit my schedule, so it seemed like everything would work out for me. Unfortunately, during one party I hosted at the house, some people ended up stealing things from my mom's friend's house, and I was asked to leave. I found a downstairs walk-out with a 1-bedroom to rent, saved enough money to buy a used car and moved out.

During my time at MLM, there was a janitor that some of us were friendly with. One day, I arrived at work, and saw that there were news vans surrounding the building. It turned out that this janitor had been arrested for allegedly killing his wife. Everyone who worked there was shocked! He seemed so nice and so normal. A year or so later, I was in the dietary office working, and the phone rang. I picked it up, and the voice on the other end said, "May I please speak to Connie?" my co-worker at the time. I said that she wasn't available, it was her day off, and the person asked, "Well, who is this?" I said, "Bobby." He then said, "Hi there, it's Jim, remember me?" It turned out that it was the janitor calling from prison! Apparently, he and Connie had a thing for each other. I hung up that phone as fast as I could, and when I told Connie the next day, she just smirked at me and shrugged it off. He was convicted and sentenced shortly after that call. I was curious as I wrote this, so I did a quick Google search, but nothing came up. It was the mid-80s, after all!

I worked at MLM for three years, interviewing people and looking at their medical intakes before suggesting a medical diet for the head Registered Dietician to review. Once again, I liked the people that I worked with but hated the all-white nursing uniform and occasional hair nets worn that were mandatory when in the kitchen. As usual, I was getting bored, and it was soon time to move on from both my job and where I lived at this time, I found an ad offering free housing, all benefits at not quite double the salary, working for the State of Minnesota as a primary caretaker for a 17-year female that was a ward of the state. I was hired, along with one other female, and while the ward, JA., lived in the entire upstairs of the house.

While I had almost completely stopped doing drugs when I stopped modeling, I was still socially drinking and started purging regularly to keep my weight in check. One afternoon, a friend and I crashed an event at the St. Paul Athletic Club, and we ran into a couple of cute guys. One asked me to dance, and I declined, and the other J. grabbed my hand, insisted on dancing with me, and dragged me out on the dance floor. Little did I know at the time, but J. would soon become my fiancé.

My roommate, S., was my age and we became good friends. We partied socially together, overall got along fine. I had my own bedroom, so there was privacy. The arrangement was that I worked from 8–4 p.m. together with S., and then one weekend a month I had to stay upstairs with JA., and then another weekend a month, I had to be on call for any emergencies. JA. had some mental health issues, and sometimes, she was violent. Other times she was depressed and suicidal. Most of the time, we hung out with her taking her to the mall to shop, to the movies, to her doctor and therapist appointments, and to get groceries, all while the state was paying for these activities, gas, and other expenses. To me, she was an annoying younger acquaintance who begged me to buy her cigarettes or beer, which I was forbidden to do. Many times, JA. pushed back by trying to run away from the house, so I would have to befriend her and promise her a special outing to come back. Other times, she refused to take her medication, and I would have to cajole her into doing so, once again offering her soda or a sweet treat. Close to a year into the job, JA. overdosed by taking all of the medication in all of her pill bottles, as was often the case, and I had to call the ambulance. They gave her syrup of ipecac to induce vomiting, and they also pumped her stomach out, and she was admitted to the hospital for three days on suicide watch. When J. was released, she came home with more meds. She later personally told me it was more of an attempt for attention rather than to take her own life. Shortly after, JA. had a violent mental breakdown and had somehow gotten hold of a knife and slit her wrists while both S. and I had the weekend off. Once again, she was taken away by ambulance. While she survived, this time, she would not be returning home, she would be admitted to a facility permanently, and once again, I was out of a job and a place to live.

    I did what I thought was normal at the time and moved in with my fiancé J. While it would be several years before I worked again, I did have many internships as part of my bachelor's degree program. I assisted by doing research on women's health, specifically looking at exercise and its effects on menstruation for Melpomene Institute. During my clinical nutrition internships I worked at North Memorial Hospital doing rounds in pediatrics, obstetrics, and gynecology. At the Veterans Administration Hospital I did rounds with radiology and oncology patients, many of whom were men still suffering the effects of WWII or the Vietnam War. But my favorite rotation was at United Hospital seeing patients in cardiology, cardiac rehabilitation, and cardiac surgery. At United I was even able to stand at the head of several open-heart surgeries to see the effects of what lack of exercise and poor diet could do to the heart. After the surgery, I was able to work with the patients on nutritional changes to their diets moving forward. As part of their cardiac rehab program, I applied the Bruce Stress Protocol, an exercise endurance test on a treadmill, to evaluate cardiac function. Speed and gradient on the treadmill are increased at intervals, and patients are hooked up to 12 point cardiac (ECG) leads to measure VO2 max (oxygen uptake), cardiac heartbeats, rhythm, and strength and timing of the heartbeat by evaluating a strip reading of the leads during and after the test.

Marriage

> "How can a woman be expected to be happy with a man who insists on treating her as if she were a perfectly normal human being."
>
> —Oscar Wilde

This section heading is called marriage, but really, many of the stories are cycles from past love relationships. I sacrificed a little piece of Spirit in each and every one of my relationships with men, whether they were one-night stands or longer affairs. Most of the time, I felt like a zombie walking around, just going through the motions. Lifeless, rote, boring, meaningless. I craved the fast-paced love affair riding the high of the honeymoon phase but wanting that honeymoon phase to never end. This, of course, is unsustainable, and I placed high expectations on all the partners I was with.

I was that girl/woman searching for something always a bit better. Several years after high school, when meeting a friend of mine for coffee, he reminded me that in high school, I told him that I was going to marry someone rich. Every time I waltzed into a new relationship, one that I forced, it was like I was stepping into a gilded prison.

I was never stable enough up to this point to hold a full-time job or even a part-time job long enough to support myself financially for more than a year or two or to make me self-sufficient. So I have always looked to someone else as a plan B, or a backup, due to not trusting in my abilities to make ends meet without being a mitigated disaster, being homeless, or living in poverty. As a result, I married the first person that I was able to bully, convince and pressure to marry me because I felt he was safe. J. felt safe emotionally, I could control him. Safe financially, he was a good provider, and it got better year after year. Safe for me to be selfish around; I did not have to be with him on a daily basis, as he traveled a lot for business, so I could do my own things. Safe that he could provide me with things I could not provide myself, travel, advanced graduate education, jewelry, and furs. Safe for extended family, he came from a normal blue-collar family with a strong connection to his three siblings. Safe because he loved me, forsaken his pregnant girlfriend for me by telling her he was gay and that she should abort the baby. She didn't, but she did give her up for adoption. Notice that while I pretended to love him for all of these safe reasons, I was not truly *in love* with him because I refused to accept this part of him.

I got engaged after two months of knowing J. I pressured him so much that he proposed to me in the jewelry store, picking up the ring. We moved in with each other shortly thereafter. I loved playing house. But by this time, my feminine instincts were no longer intact. I had no idea how to break off this engagement. If you were raised with the trauma of poverty and unmothered like I was, with a mother that was not in touch with Soul, not present, just busy, how could I possibly stand a chance to listen and believe my intuition?

Walking down the aisle in Borlange, Sweden, on June 29th, 1990, wearing the state crown jewels on my head, with around 40 relatives in attendance, I once again fooled myself. I knew instinctively that I should run. However, I went through with the fairy tale marriage of being saved and my newfound status of being married. I was also fooled by the desire to be loved and accepted. I knew that I would not be able to live fully in Soul, but rather I would always be in the shadow of this person. At the age of 25, I had already been so cut off and separated from Soul for the past nine years; I did not see the error in following my ego. The reality of my thoughts was rationalization: "It's really not bad that he is/or did_____." Bottom line, I romanticized the wedding and the *prince*, and I naively made an extremely poor choice. Not to say that he wasn't a good husband and, later, a good father, but he was not my person. Marriage, to me, was a validation from society. I knew that my inner knowing was buried and had not been used since the trauma of my move out of poverty and that even today, I still struggle with listening to myself. At times of importance, my instincts tended to pop up, but as a conditioned human Being, I ignored them and went with what I perceived or assumed was right at that time. This not listening to my deep knowing, like so many other times when I did not listen to myself, often resulted in a disastrous ending.

To the outer world, I was a beautiful, smart, successful, happy woman, and I played favorites with my outer self, ignoring inner Spirit. I was distracted with life, not willing to dig deeper, being anti-deep consciousness, and not paying attention at all to Soul. This loss of consciousness was me paying attention to the wrong reality. It was an addiction to the fantasy of forcing the shoe to fit and hoping for the best. The one thing that I always had going for me was my drive to never give up, and I kept trying to figure out things until I got to true Soul work. I turned within to the deepest depths, where Soul's Light could be seen and felt. I needed to prioritize and focus, and as you had read earlier, I fought for my inner life to come alive again. These distractions that I spent years on fed the pain cycle I was in and hindered my growth.

I was so sad during this time, even while being surrounded by all the material things in life: a private plane, diamonds, furs, Louis Vuitton bags, etc. I was seduced by the illusion of having outward things and luxury surrounding me that would temporarily make me happy. But only for a brief time, as soon as the object of my desire was bought; the happiness wore off, and I was once back into deep sadness. I was like a child that acted a certain way to get what they wanted. All the while, my wild warrior wanted to be free to live and be authentically me.

At some point, I wanted to escape. Most people do this through alcohol or drugs, and I did as well, but I also did this through promiscuity. This has been my destructive modus operandi (M.O.), as I have always tried external outward displays of flirting towards the opposite sex in hopes of getting caught so at least I would get some attention. I did not want to take a cold hard look in the mirror because the work I would have to do on myself would be too hard. I was searching for ANYTHING that would make me feel alive again.

I began to sneak. I snuck into the bathroom to vomit, and my bulimia became bad for a few years in my marriage. I snuck out to meet friends and grab time away from J., eventually sneaking out to meet exciting new men. I snuck in fantasy time, reading about or daydreaming about the life I really was born to live. It was just another way of tricking myself to be happy. I was trying to set myself free, but the things I was seeking weren't good for me. But when you sneak around and follow others' paths, eventually, you will get caught, and things will blow up. I was living off the bare minimum of human connection from my husband.

I knew I *had to* stay in the marriage for my parents, for my faith, for my children. I would continue to put on a brave face of happiness and the perfect marriage, husband, and children, all the while I was escaping into this other world of fantasy lovers. In many ways, I thought I was tricking my husband, and I was just waiting for a time that I would become strong, and he would be weak, and then I would strike and run to escape. This was my wise inner woman rising up without me knowing it, calling upon all of the masculine energy inside of me, using instinctual rage against him to fight for my release. I was not to be caged any longer. But I was looking for love in all the wrong places, as the song goes. I was looking to others for love, and I should have been looking internally to heal myself. But this almost compulsive type of behavior would continue on for decades.

For years in this marriage, I was on the hamster wheel of keeping up with the Joneses. I lived a less authentic life and did not live the best, most fulfilled life. I was so attention to detail oriented and had to have everything perfect. I obsessively cleaned, on my hands and knees, with a toothbrush around the corners of a new house. What I should have been cleansing was inner Spirit, mind, and body with that rigor to help renourish Soul. I should have asked my Spirit guides for help to sweep and whisk away all of my pain and conditioning and spent more time living for myself, learning to heal, and doing what I wanted to do on my Spiritual path. In the truest sense, I had lost my fire, my passion, and therefore, myself. Every action I was taking was not for myself or Spirit, but for others. Without this passion, the nasty things of the ego come to light, and I spent all my days on minutiae and unimportant tasks, accomplishments, and gaining material goods. I became an outwardly nice, trying too hard, a very fake, subdued person. Tempering my wild child yet acting out privately.

I was bored and needed a challenge. So I signed up for the Mrs. Minnesota pageant. I worked with a coach, K. I tanned, worked out, took my measurements trying to reduce them and my weight, practiced speaking and walking, learned about current events, tried on gowns, shoes, and jewelry, found sponsors to help pay for it all and ended up being 2nd runner up or third place finisher.

I also decided I needed to get back to work. A friend of mine mentioned that there was a job opening downtown from most of my runway auditions, selling bridal gowns at Barbara's Bridals and Milton's, part-time on nights and weekends and that it paid both hourly and commission. This sounded like a fun job! I applied, got the job, and started shortly after. All brides and their moms and bridal parties are in a good mood when first coming in to try on gowns. However, the bridal gown sale cycle did not result in an immediate purchase. Often it took 2–3 times more appointments. What made me successful at selling gowns was being able to flatter the bride, show dresses within the parents' price range, and listen to what the bride was looking for and evaluate the bride's shape to make sure the dress was flattering. I remember many months being the number one salesperson, and on Saturday appointments, regularly winning the $100-$200 cash prize at the end of the day. I stayed in this job for around 2 ½ years, and I only left after I was married and got pregnant with my son because we were moving to Mankato, MN.

Right after I got engaged, my mother-in-law gave me a shoot of a *Hoya Carnosa* plant that she smuggled over from Sweden in a tampon box. It was so precious to me. This little shoot grew and grew as I kept repotting it and tending to it. I felt that I needed to really take care of this plant, as it was so precious to me. This species of *Hoya* typically can take 5–7 years to bloom; however, I think mine took more like nine years. By the time we moved into our newly constructed lake house, it had vines that reached six feet to the ground. It would bloom only at night and be so fragrant that you could smell it in the house for days on end. When we moved to MA and moved the Hoya, eventually, the leaves started falling off and it never bloomed again. For this reason, I will forever associate plants with the relationships in my life, for it was at this time that my marriage started dying, and there was no reviving it.

Children

> "Children are like wet cement. Whatever falls on them makes an impression."
>
> —*Haim Ginott*

> "To raise a child, who is comfortable enough to leave you, means you've done your job. They are not ours to keep but to teach them to soar on their own."
>
> —*Anonymous*

When each of my children was born, once again, my mother-in-law gave me a plant shoot to mark the occasion. She stole a piece of a corn plant in the same hospital where they were born. Once again, I tended and nurtured each of these plants as my life depended on them. When I got divorced, I neglected them, which ended up being a metaphor for my parenting. Eventually, both those plants would die, mimicking the relationship with my children years later.

My son was born in 1992, the first-born grandchild into both families with six uncles. My daughter was born in 1994, and when I was in labor with her, my husband's parents, Farmor and Farfar as they are called in Swedish, took my son over the summer to their cabin on the lake for three months so I could bond with her. I am not going to write too much about my children, that is their own story to tell, but I will say for many years, we were a happy, cohesive family. They attended a small private, Catholic K-8 school together, and then both went on to same-sex Catholic High Schools: Boston College High School in Dorchester and Notre Dame Academy in Hingham. Both were in numerous after-school activities: chess club, basketball, ski club, swimming, and scouting. My son received his Eagle Scout medal with palms at 14 years old, and my daughter received her Gold Award at 16. Both were scouted for swimming scholarships for college. My son chose the College of St. Rose in Albany, NY, and graduated with a degree in Communications. My daughter chose Pepperdine University in Malibu, CA, and graduated in three years with a degree in Film. Both are well on their way to having well-established careers by following their own path.

I found out I was pregnant again around two years after my daughter was born. I knew I was so unhappy in my marriage that I could not bear to have or raise another child. So I went to my Dr. to take the morning-after pill, which were two tablets that would induce labor. It didn't work. I was beside myself, ruminating on what harm I had caused this unborn child. Would it be born with birth defects? Would I be forever scared by my decision? Not knowing does not offer proper protection or all the facts to make an informed decision. But this is where my intellectual mind won over my intuition. I knew that it wasn't right to have this baby. This would be a continuous loop of not listening to what was left of Soul and just staying in the comfort zone of my life. A week later, I started bleeding and soon after that, I went to the Doctor's office to get a complete dilation and curettage (D & C). Shame once again set in for years.

I was always so concerned with what others thought of us. I wanted to appear to have the perfect marriage and the perfect children. In the process of conforming to societal norms, I did not align with my children's Spirit and what was right for them. I molded them into what I thought would look "right" on the outside, not caring what was right for them on the inside. I feared not fitting in or being an outcast, mimicking a teenager wanting to be part of *the* cool group of people. It was not about my children but about self-preservation for me in the world.

Like most moms, I was also very protective; a momma bear, if you will. I was always so scared that something bad was going to happen to them that I ended up intervening in every little problem (and some big problems), never allowing them to learn the lesson or figure out things for themselves. I believe I was also very nurturing, providing them with great birthdays, holidays, and traditional experiences carried down from our Swedish and Prussian cultures. I loved getting hugs and kisses from them and wanted them to make the most of their young lives.

But I could also be a very cold, stern, angry, steely mother with my children. I never gave them the benefit of the doubt and always pushed them way beyond their limits. While I am Caucasian, I fit the mold of the stereotypical Tiger mom, but in my case, I was a fire-breathing Dragon mom. I would rage at them, show anger if I could not control things, and in hindsight, I realize that my children were sensitive to this. They had a gentler constitution than I had. I was already toughened up by then, and they had not yet gone through any of life's difficulties. I also had such elevated expectations for my kids and was never happy with what they achieved. I always wanted them to do more, do better, and climb higher. I know this stems from what I have gone through in my life and what I have overcome. I was driven, so I wanted my kids to be as well.

I poured heart, Soul, and everything I had into micromanaging and raising my children. I was the perfect soccer mom. As mentioned earlier, carpooling to Scouts, chess club, skiing, swimming, drama, my kids were in everything. I recognize, in hindsight, that I pushed my kids to do things so that I could fill the void of my life with being busy. I became codependent with them, enmeshed in their Beings. I was the best mother that I knew how to be. But like all of my relationships, I tended to give too much of myself to them.

Part of the façade was when we traveled to faraway exotic locations for weeks on end as a family. Egypt, Africa, China, Japan, and Europe. It was like an urgent thirst for me to see new countries, rushing frantically around, dragging my husband and kids behind me, never stopping in any one city long enough to enjoy the present moment. Oh, we checked off every one of the must "sees" in the travel guide books, and the wilder the excursion, I made sure we were booked on it. Hot balloon rides over the Serengeti? Check. Visiting the white-faced Geishas in Kyoto? Yes. Christmas Eve, traveling by camel over a desert to visit the Tomb of Kings in Egypt? Of course. There were no trips that would not earn me bragging rights back home. As a result, my children don't really travel. We were on the go constantly, so much so that there was no down time. My kids were already drained and tired at an early age because of my insecurities.

As a parent, I now realize I did great harm to my kids, not in a physical or sexual way, but in a Soulful, emotional way. Time after time, I did psychic surgery on them, trying to cut away at the parts that made them who they were in order to fit into my expectations of who they should be, perfect children. Isn't that what my father tried to do to me? In essence, I was trying to reconfigure their Souls into something that they weren't. The pressure that my children felt must have been immeasurable. That, coupled with the hours of homework they would have each night, and the 3–4 hours of swim practice they would endure, caused them to be so stifled. So much so that now as adults, they both keep me at arm's length: my son emotionally by not seeing me for going on three years now, and my daughter physically as she lived in Hawaii, and just recently moved back to LA. Before Covid hit, my son cut me off. He stopped talking to me, seeing me, and blocked all and every kind of communication. We have reestablished calls on the phone, on birthdays and holidays, and I have hope that slowly and respectfully, we can once again restore our adult relationship. My daughter recently stayed with me for three weeks. I thought she treated me horribly. She thought I was mean, a horrible mom, and a toxic parent. These are recent sentiments. During this stay, after a big blow-up, she needed my help as she was in a vulnerable position. I helped her with no judgment, and the next day I told her how I struggled with being in that same position. I am hoping that because of this experience, we both can see each other in new, more compassionate ways and that we will continue to heal this relationship as well. Update: my daughter and I are back on track and my son and I recently had an hour long Zoom call to catch up. I was asked to write a chapter in an anthology about motherhood called *Motherhood. Unfiltered*. I ended up writing in-depth from my perspective of a mother who experiences estrangement from her adult child.

I think they are both afraid of me in their own different ways. I think they both feel that they could never keep up with my achievements, that they are afraid of disappointing me and my wrath of only being adequate, not stellar, and of me stifling their Souls. Thankfully, they retained some of their spark and most of their Spirit, never becoming the compliant adolescents or adults that had *soulless*, shallow looks. Both rebelled in their own ways, although it took them much later in life to do so.

I love them with all my heart and Soul. I did the best I could, with the best I knew, at the time. I just was not living in my Divine feminine, loving Spirit, but from a Divine masculine, stern, triggered individual. Would I go back and change things? Absolutely! But I know deep in Soul I was, and sometimes still am, in survival and protection mode most of the time and that I did not have the capacity for empathy, play, or joy when raising them. I know better and am a different person now. I hope one day, they both will be able to see this change in me and forgive me.

More Schooling

> "An investment in knowledge pays the best interest."
> —Benjamin Franklin

I graduated from the College of Saint Catherine with a Bachelor of Arts degree, with a concentration in a program that I designed, Exercise Science. I was so mesmerized by my experiences at United Hospital and the cardiac program that I determined I would pursue a master's degree immediately in this field. I filled out my application to Mankato State University (MSU) and was accepted and enrolled in a 2-year program with another year allocated to research.

While in school for my master's degree in Mankato, I already had a 1-year-old at home, and one year into my program was pregnant with my second child. I was so busy as a young mom with my husband traveling all the time, but I knew that I also needed to get out of the house. I decided to take a part-time job at a jewelry store in the local mall, hoping to combine the staff discount towards my love of diamonds. I purchased many rings, necklaces, earrings, and other items during my three years at Williams Diamond Center, all while learning all there was to know about the 4 Cs of a diamond: cut, clarity, color, and carat. Once again, this paid hourly and on commission, and I so enjoyed the thrill of making my goals and being the number one salesperson monthly, quarterly, and then yearly. north

In the summer between my first and second year of my master's program, a front-page local newspaper article came out about my successful modeling career and Mrs. Minnesota pageant experience, in which I placed 2nd runner up. Soon after, I received a call from Georgene Brock, Director of Women's Athletics at MSU. She had seen the article, and knew I was attending graduate school and wondered if I might be interested in coaching the new women's dance team, which for the first time would be in competition as a Division 1 sports team. Georgene had been working hard since 1966 to offset the gender inequity that women had faced while participating in sports at MSU. In 1995, she officially added three sports to the women's Division 1 program: dance team, junior varsity volleyball, and women's soccer satisfying the Office Civil Rights gender equality standards (45% to 55% with the men's programs). I jumped at the chance to be the first coach, and this was mentioned in the *MSU Reporter* on September 14th, 1995. It paid a small stipend, and due to my schedule, practices were often at 5 a.m. or 7 p.m., and it saddens me to this day that I only lasted at this job for one semester. The hours, my other job, the classes, and my children all started to take its toll on me, and I soon resigned. I will forever be grateful to Georgene for giving me this opportunity, and I regret not being able to take on this role for any length of time.

In my childhood, I was featured in the local paper a lot during that time. I was dropping my children off at their school one morning, and I received a frantic call from my husband at the time. He asked me where I was, and I immediately thought he had been in a car accident and hurt. I told him that I was in the school parking lot and I had just dropped the kids off. He told me sternly, "Stay right there. Don't go anywhere. The police will be there in a few minutes." Now I was really worried. The officers pulled up and calmly asked me to follow them to the station. I did as I was told, and once inside, they finally told me what was happening. Evidently, weeks prior, there was a man who ran his wife over with a boat, killing her. During the investigation, they found newspaper clippings of various news articles in his home about me! They wanted to see if I knew him, recognized him, and what my day-to-day habits were. I had never seen or met him, nor did I recognize him. The officers told me that they thought he had been following me as the newspaper articles had said I was a professor at Mankato State University, and mentioned other activities that I participated in. It was super scary to think I had a stalker and wasn't even aware of it! He was convicted of the crime and was sentenced to life in prison. Out of curiosity, I once again did a quick Google search and found out his conviction was just recently overturned and that he was out of jail after 25 years! Thankfully, I live on the other side of the country now. This was the first stalking experience with someone I didn't know, but sadly it wouldn't be the last. I had a boyfriend after my divorce that, even after we broke up, would continue to "show up" at places claiming to randomly run into me. One day I was teaching at my University, and I looked out the window, and he was standing outside my classroom! Last I heard, he had gotten married, and I never saw or heard from him again.

Also, during my second year in the master's program, I was offered a graduate stipend to help pay for my classes and a position teaching the laboratory portion of both a biomechanics and a kinesiology course as a graduate assistant. I left William's Diamonds and fell in love with teaching and being center stage. Throughout the year, I developed mini-lectures, graded lab homework, and assigned grades, all the while finishing up my course work. As part of the program at MSU, we were required to write a formal thesis on a topic, as well as to present our findings to fellow graduate students and defend them to our committee consisting of three other professors, Dr. K. Ecker, Dr. M. Visser, and Dr. N. Williams.

I was the first of my classmates to complete my dissertation, and my defense was scheduled for early May. My mom had been diagnosed with breast and ovarian cancer several years prior, and she was currently in hospice. My family had just spent Mother's Day with her in the facility, and she appeared to be doing as well as could be expected. The night before my defense, I was particularly anxious. I decided to give my dad a call, as he could always give me the validation I needed and, for the most part, calm me down. As soon as I called him, I was on even higher alert. He sounded distant and unlike himself. I pushed and pushed, asking him what was wrong, and he finally broke down to tell me that my mom had passed away that evening, May 7th, 1996, and that he did not want to tell me because he knew it would affect my presentation the next day. Immediately I considered canceling and rescheduling it. He told me it would not have been what my mom would have wanted; she would have wanted me to go through with the thesis defense, that she loved me and was so proud of me. My dad reminded me that there was nothing I could do the next day, so he urged me to move forward. The next afternoon, I was in shock, not getting much sleep. I walked into the auditorium and gave my presentation. I received some push back and challenging questions from professors, and I answered back calmly, not caring if I passed or not. I left the room along with all the other students watching, so the committee could make their decision. As soon as I stepped into the hallway, I broke down sobbing hysterically. My friends thought it was because of some tough questions that were thrown my way. When my committee chair came to get me and saw me crying, I had to explain to everyone that my mom had just died the night before. Everyone seemed surprised that I was able to pull it together and be so rational. After all this, I found out I had passed both my written (given the week before) and oral examinations. Finally, my original research, titled *The Effects of Conditioning and Gender on Ratings of Perceived Exertion During Physical Exercise*, was to be hard copy bound. I was able to put in a dedication to my mom and also my dad on the first page before it went to press:

"In memory of my mother, who has shown me that the true challenge in life is to persevere. For her patience, devotion, and willingness to live a full and rewarding life.

To my father, who has given me my sense of humor; to be able to laugh and find the fun in everyday situations. They both have always shown me great support, understanding, and love as I plodded through the trials and tribulations of my own life. Thanks for making me who I am today. I love you very much."

—*Dedication from The Effects of Conditioning and Gender on Ratings of Perceived Exertion During Physical Exercise, 1996.*

To this day, my thesis can be found in the stacks of the MSU library and its archives and in several University libraries across the U.S. I graduated on June 7th, 1996, with a Master of Science, Exercise Physiology concentration.

I fell into teaching business by happenstance. I have always loved the sciences and thought that I would eventually go to medical school. But after I graduated, I had a friend who taught at the College of Business call me up and ask if I would be interested in substituting out the semester for a professor that was out sick, taking over his graduate-level Organizational Theory and Design class. First, I thought, "Business? I don't know the first thing about business!" Then, I realized this was strictly a theory course, with the information taken right out of the textbook, I realized I could manage it. I was always up for a new challenge. I applied, and due to the fact that I was already lecturing at the college, I got the job. I was extremely nervous walking into that classroom the first time, and I was a bit out of my element, yet prepared. I had worked so hard on PowerPoints and what I was going to lecture on. At that time, the average graduate student demographic still tended to be majority male, early 30s to mid-40s many of them working full time at Fortune 500 companies in the area, with those organizations paying for these leaders to receive their MBAs. Imagine me at 28 with absolutely no business experience to speak of, teaching a bunch of mid-level male managers about this! However, I fell so in love with the topic that I decided, right then and there, to switch career paths after graduation.

It didn't quite happen as I had hoped, and I ended up teaching at MSU in the business school for almost four years. I taught management classes, and organizational behavior classes and it was this last class that sparked my interest to apply to a doctorate program at St. Mary's University. I was accepted and immediately enrolled in a Leadership program with an emphasis in Organizational Behavior. Classes were held in cohort-type fashion, with one group being the Mankato cohort; there were 11 of us that first started out. Our schedules were jammed packed with learning, testing, and papers, and as you can imagine, I was constantly spreading myself too thin. During this time, my husband and I had a highly active social life with friends, belonged to a dinner and dance club, church groups, and bridge card playing group (me), and I even was initiated into a service sorority, Beta Sigma Phi: Delta Zeta Chapter 11053. To say it was challenging was an understatement, yet I thrived.

In addition to all this crazy activity, I was asked for my advice on some business dealings and got paid for it. Mind you, I only had theoretical knowledge, but my husband would ask my advice for his company, and sometimes a manager in my class that I was teaching would seek me out. One of those managers happened to work for General Motors, and I was offered my business opinion about a merger and acquisition deal that had happened, and his department was struggling with a culture change with international employees. Unbeknownst to me, this was the unofficial start of my consulting career. I wrote up a report after doing an organizational assessment and was given a rather large check at the time for my efforts. The entire project lasted mere months, but one of the perks I still have to this day is that when I rent a car from National Rental Car, I still enjoy the Emerald Aisle as a past GM contract employee.

Two years into this three-year program, my husband J. came home from traveling and told me that they were either transferring him to the West or East Coast and asked if I had a preference. We both had lots of family and spent a lot of time in California, and I knew the University and school systems were great on the East Coast, so that's where my vote went. We had just gotten done building a custom four-bedroom, post, and beam construction house on a large lake lot in Madison Lake, MN, so I wasn't too worried about not being able to finish up my schooling, as I assumed that it would take a while for this to sell. J. moved out to Massachusetts, and I stayed back so that the children could finish up the school year. We placed the house on the market in early August. Within two weeks received a cash offer for the full asking price with the stipulation that we move out within two weeks! The scramble was on to find a house to buy or a townhouse to rent and get the kids enrolled in a new school. My son, J.R., would be starting 2nd grade, and my daughter, Kyra, would be starting Kindergarten. I am not sure how I did it, but we rented a place, and they both were accepted into Our Lady Comforter of the Afflicted K-8 school in Waltham, MA.

Now what to do about my schooling? After a few hours of research on the Internet, the closest program that would align with the one at St. Mary's was a similar one at Boston College (BC). I started the application process and set up a meeting with the admissions counselor. I met with someone in late August and thought all I had to complete was nine more months of classes. I was soon told, in no uncertain terms, that BC had a residency requirement, which by only a handful of my courses would transfer over. This would set me back at least a year and a half. To me this was outrageous. I couldn't wait that long, not to mention the cost of the increased tuition. So I discussed it with J, and he talked to the C-levels in the company, and they granted him a 9-month paid sabbatical to work from home on most days. I re-enrolled in classes that December, and every Monday morning, I would fly out of Logan Airport (BOS) on a 5:00 a.m. Delta flight to Minneapolis (MPS) to start my day. I would rent a car and stay in a dorm room for alumni on St. Kate's campus and then fly back home late Wednesday evening after my classes. I did this for the next six months. When summer came, everyone moved back to stay with my in-laws at their lake home in Hayward, northern Wisconsin. I moved down to Winona, MN, to stay in the dorms to take as many day and night classes as I could to finish up before September. I remember only seeing J. and my children one time in that three-month period, I was so busy, and when I finally went to sleep, it was many times too late to call them.

We all were back together in Waltham in late August, as I had finally accomplished what I set out to do. I finished my classwork and started on my dissertation. I needed access to any University library, and I would have to fly back for my written cumulative testing and oral examination, but for the research, I could work from home. I re-contacted the Department Chair at the Carroll School of Management at BC and explained my situation. She granted me reciprocity to use the library and take out books if I needed to. I also contacted the librarian at Bentley College, who gave me permission to use that library. I passed both my written and oral exams in the next month and went to work writing and researching my dissertation topic, which was on the leadership qualities within the Catholic Church. I sent out surveys to hundreds of priests throughout the United States, polling them on what leadership attributes they felt best served them and the parishioners of their parishes. Most people don't understand that the Catholic Church is run as a highly profitable organization, with the CEO being the Pope, the Board of Directors being the Cardinals, the Vice Presidents being the Bishops, and the managers being the parish Priests. After one year of writing every day, I was ready to defend my dissertation. As with my thesis, my committee of 4 (Dr. J. Moye, Dr. R. Eubank, Dr. W. Kelly, and Dr. P. Sheedy) asked some tough questions, and one member being a stickler over a single word choice that I had written, but as soon as I agreed to change that word, I was approved, and the *Preferred Leadership Practices of a Religious Organization* was published. I graduated in December 2004 from St. Mary's University with a doctorate in Leadership with a concentration in Organizational Behavior. I was now to be called Dr. Roberta A. Pellant and proudly wore the rounded Tudor bonnet with tassel when I walked at graduation on January 23rd, 2005.

Divorce

"You know why divorcesv are so expensive?
Because they're worth it."
—*Willie Nelson*

A woman can only go along living with the perfect life, husband, children, house, etc., for so long before it starts to suck the life out of her and strangle her. I completely lost the urge to be independent, creative and work on my own personal development. Dead inside. I censored and hid what

I saw and *knew* to be true, tucked it deep in some unknown corner, and pretended that it wasn't there. To forget it, I became delusional, resentful, and greedy. And for many years, I stuffed it down, 20 years to be exact. Soul was starving, missing the pieces of itself, and I could not stand it any longer. Why did it take me this long to recognize the dampening or forgetting of Soul?

I have always been on my own path. But I have also always stopped and taken detours, dragging others along with me. In most, if not all, of my relationships, I have expected and required them to be something they are not, to do things they don't want to do, failing to honor and respect their desires along the way. My marriage was no different. No human being could live up to the unrealistic high expectations I had in my marriage. But gosh, did he try.

In 2005, my father was diagnosed with stage 4 colon cancer. He had an easy transition and end to this lifetime experience. I don't believe it is a coincidence that it was only after my father died in 2006, that I filed for a separation in 2007, and finally, I was divorced in 2008. It was like I waited to do so, so as not to disappoint him with a failed marriage.

I was divorced rather quickly, but afterwards I went through a stressful 5-year on and off again court battle with my ex-husband based on various issues not being upheld in our divorce decree. He moved out of our house and moved in with a much younger girlfriend he worked with who adored him, so it was easy for him. It was easy for me to end it because I wanted a different relationship with *anyone* other than him, not only due to who we were together but also due to the financial Internal Revenue System (I.R.S.) back tax liens that were incurred solely because of his unilateral decisions. I have to say that because there was a third person in the mix of the financials, I wholeheartedly now know that he was not 100% to blame for some of the guilty contempt judgments issued against him. I do believe he was responsible for allowing someone else to have control of his finances. In stereotypical fashion, I was made out to be the villain, and everything was blamed on me. My ex-mother-in-law talked so poorly about me and made up so many untruths about me during this tough time that looking back at what was said is comical. I have to say thank you to my brothers-in-law (his brothers) for their love and support of me and the children during this time. I am sure it was not easy to do. I am willing to take responsibility for not being the best wife in the marriage. However, I will not take one shred of responsibility for the financial disaster created during the divorce and afterward. Once again, I had gone from "riches to rags." I walked away with $130 per week in alimony from an almost 20-year marriage.

Recently, I just heard from one of my sisters-in-law that even now, 15 years later, my mother-in-law is still vilifying me by spreading lies and rumors about me and my parenting. I have to laugh, as I don't wish one iota of ill will upon this person. How does that saying go? "If you are talking about me, I appreciate the advertisement?"

Consulting and Entrepreneurship

> "If it is to be, it is up to me."
> —William Johnsen

I was burnt out. I needed to take some time off from battling through the separation and did just that. After a year of catching my breath, I was ready to put my CV or resume for academics out in the Universe and started applying for University jobs. I was fortunate enough to be granted an interview and a guest lecturing evaluation from the Management department at Bentley University and was soon hired as an Adjunct Professor for their MBA program in June 2006.

I was expected to get a full-time job after my divorce, as Massachusetts imputes income on the wife after being granted a divorce. While I was working as a professor at the end of this time, I was still only receiving around $130 a week in alimony. I did receive just enough child support to keep my kids in their private schools and activities. But I was still so very dependent on my ex-husband. At first, I set my hourly consulting rate at $200, and the more work I started receiving, over time, I slowly increased my prices to $400 an hour. Most of the time, for larger projects, I would charge a flat fee of $1000-$10,000 depending on the amount of time it would take me to complete, but on average, my clients were being billed at ~$2,500-$4,500 per project, with the option to have additional hourly rates added on. Slowly but surely, I was finding my worth.

Teaching business and strategy has always been my passion. But it would not pay the bills at less than $10,000 a class, and as an adjunct, I was only teaching two classes at most a semester. I am innately a storyteller; in my mind and in person, I am always overcommunicating a lesson, or response with a story. It energizes me; it makes me light up to share my business acumen with students. I love both the left brain thought practice behind it, but I also strive to bring up the right-sided creativeness when problem-solving. Many students have told me that my eyes light up and I shine when I am teaching! I tell them that the reason I am so happy when I teach is that I can't wait to dump everything that is in my brain and what I have learned out to them. I decided to start consulting in earnest, and Roberta Pellant Consulting (RPC) was created in 2008 as a sole proprietorship.

Some of my first clients were mid-sized businesses that needed help with their marketing or business planning development. I then jumped to startup companies that needed help with management hiring, funding, and operations strategy. From there, I developed a tighter niche and worked primarily with women entrepreneurs, sharing organizational development knowledge through the creation of marketing plans and booking speaking engagements. The man, S., I was dating then, knew that I was focusing on consulting, and he introduced me to a creative female who was looking for someone to help her develop her original first-to-market product line.

I first started consulting for Bum Boosa Bamboo Products® (BBBP) in 2011, eventually transitioning into a VP of Marketing and Organizational development and principal owner. BBBP® was a woman-run, bio-based, non-woven bamboo company whose products included first-to-world market 100% bamboo baby wipes, toilet paper, bamboo powder diaper ointment, and early-stage prototyping of bamboo diapers. I helped Bum Boosa Bamboo® through the stringent process of becoming a Certified B Corporation. I loved supporting the Bum Boosa® green initiative and 100% woman-run company. I was deeply inspired by the company's environmental mission and gained product development experience while maintaining high energy and enthusiasm to move the company to the next level. I focused on communication, promotion, and pricing strategy, as well as helping implement several new successful product launches. I independently and collaboratively managed primary research efforts to support quantitative and qualitative analysis within the industry and generated comprehensive marketing plans to improve customer relationship management and grow sales. The company was being vetted for Shark Tank in 2014 due to innovation and recognition in the industry. Bum Boosa Bamboo® quickly expanded, despite only small initial funding from friends and family, and in 2018 was internationally acquired.

Immediately after this, I was contacted by a mid-sized company that was going through a merger and acquisition with a well-known larger company in an industry that I was not familiar with. I didn't really have the time to spend time learning about it. For non-disclosure agreement purposes, I can't mention the industry or the two companies involved. The mid-sized company asked me to help navigate through the process, and I did not want to do it. To be professional, I sent them a proposal, but instead of asking my normal rate of $400 an hour, I doubled it to $800, thinking they would turn it down. Well, imagine my surprise when the contract was accepted. From then on, I understood and learned to value my worth, and $800 became my new hourly rate with mid-larger-sized clients.

Corporate responsibility and sustainable efforts were gaining traction in the U.S. as more companies were interested in this topic. While I helped Bum Boosa® gain B-corporation status, I still was not well informed about what all it entailed. I decided once again to go back to school, this time post-doctorate for a 4-course professional graduate-level certificate at both Harvard Summer and Extension School. It took me three years to complete, learning about LEED certifications, reducing an organization's carbon footprint, regulatory compliance reporting, different ISO reports, zero waste packaging, and risk management. I met the requirements on June 1st, 2016, and many of my clients benefit from my knowledge in this area.

Mid-August 2019, I was released early from my teaching contract from the non-profit Year Up, an organization that educates and trains underprivileged youth to close the opportunity divide. I had no prospective clients in sight, and I would not be able to re-sign my contract with Bentley until January. I was in a panic. I had signed up to take the personal development course, Breakthrough to Success, with Jack Canfield[3] in Scottsdale, Arizona, which would be starting in a few weeks, and I thought long and hard about canceling the trip. I decided to still go. Everything was paid for except the hotel, and hopefully, I'd learn something to help me through this transition period I was going through.

Jack Canfield has written several books, most notably the *Chicken Soup for the Soul®* series and *The Success Principles*™, and as I was listening to Jack speak on the main stage, I felt like I needed to sit down and talk to him. I had paid extra to sit in the VIP lunchroom where Jack would often mingle. We were in a silent period between sessions, where

---

3. https://jackcanfield.com/

we couldn't talk but focus on reflection. As soon as he was done speaking I rushed up to the stage with a note saying, "Hi Jack, will you have lunch at my table so that I can talk to you about something?" He laughed and responded, "Maybe, it all depends on if my staff needs to prep me on things for the afternoon session." I waited patiently until lunch, grabbed my salad from the buffet, and kept a chair next to me empty for him. I was pleasantly surprised when he sought me out, and I was able to have a long conversation with him. I talked to him about my situation, my credentials, and everything I could think of to help lay the groundwork. He gave me a lot of great advice, but two things stuck in my mind. First, he told me that he and I were very much alike. We both worked our way up the ranks in the education field and became successful business owners. He told me that, in his mind, we were colleagues and that I could do anything I put my mind to. The second thing he advised me to do was stop marketing to one-on-one consulting clients. I should develop workshops and do corporate training and charge between $10,000 and $25,000+ per workshop. This was incredibly sage advice! The best opportunity I had at this event was to network with other people regarding this while asking them if they could help. I used every opportunity from then on to tell my story and ask people for help. One gentleman, Jesse, asked me for a card and said that his company was looking for some training. Less than six weeks later, I did a half-day C-level corporate training for Aimia in Minneapolis, MN, and the money I received for this workshop held me over until my teaching paycheck in early February. I haven't looked back since.

Years later, I was fortunate to be invited to Jack's house in Santa Barbara, where he interviewed me on his television show, *Talking about Success*. I was in the process of developing and writing the book with a colleague, *Business Capital 101*, and happened to tell Jack the story of how grateful I was for his advice. He smiled and told me to keep on focusing on what I wanted, to take action, and most of all, act *as if;* as if I was already where I wanted to be in my life. I am so grateful for him, his recommendation on my LinkedIn profile, getting to spend time with him and his wife, Inga, in Costa Rica, and for all his mentorship, training, books, and seminars I have attended over the past several years. I would highly recommend the Canfield Training Group to anyone that feels like they are stuck in a rut. Jack knows how to motivate people and helps them dream big.

Throughout the years, I have worked with several female start-up clients such as: Shop WITH Bags and Just Bee & Me, and in 2016 I met an owner of several smaller inns who already had been in business for 25 years. I was originally hired as a consultant to help with the growing businesses' marketing needs, and then transitioned into helping with reservations and guest services, tracking the finances monthly, and making sure that the financial success of the business was sustained. I advised on booking pace, room pricing, event planning, promotional and social media marketing, reputation management, quarterly and yearly goals for the properties. But my most significant contribution to date would have to be, without a doubt, the fact that during COVID, I increased revenue for the properties. During this time, the hospitality industry was hit hard. On March 17th, 2020, the inns were temporarily closed. When the state finally gave the go-ahead to reopen on June 1st, 2020, in an effort to make up for lost revenue and, to get more customers in the door, the owner instinctively, out of fear, decreased the prices. They were adamant about doing this, and all I could do was silently step back and watch, even though I had a feeling it wouldn't work. It didn't, and within one month, cancellations were coming in at an even more alarming rate. Based on my knowledge of fear, I suggested that the business *raise* the room rates. After all, what did we have to lose? What the owner was doing was struggling against failure. The increased prices piqued people's interest, establishing the business as having a luxury brand. Lo and behold, at the end of 2020, I was able to increase the payments brought in by 2.3% over the previous year, 2019. In 2021, I increased revenue by 29%

over 2020, and in 2022 I increased revenue by 4.4% over 2021. I talked about this in my TEDx talk, "I Want You to Fail."

For almost 16 years, I have taught at Bentley University across three different departments: Management, Marketing and Informational Design, and Corporate Communication. I have gained extensive experience in developing new curriculum, receiving accreditation for those new classes, and was an early adopter of instituting online learning across several platforms long before COVID. Additionally, I have been honored to be a Visiting Professor at Newbury College, Boston College, Clark University, Year Up, a non-profit organization that serves underprivileged youth, allowing them to gain college credits for classes, as well as internationally at Cracow School of Business, and Warsaw Akademia, Poland. I have taught 24 (!) different courses at both the undergraduate and graduate levels, including teaching and helping in the development of the Bentley Corporate Immersion Institute, which offers classes whereby the students offer consulting services based on the client's need to start-up companies and entrepreneurs. I have acted as a Project Manager Professor to student teams in the course Integrated Business Functions, a specialized corporate immersion undergraduate class. In six out of seven semesters, a student team in my section won the Distinguished Harnett Business Plan Award, given to the most comprehensive business plan, incorporating the best ideas for development for an organization, which was independently voted on by four faculty members along with respective company representatives for whom the plan was written for. This is a monetary award matched by the businesses. Corporate partnerships have included: Brave Hearts Amazon launch, IBIS, Virtual High School, Aniello, Mary Lou's Coffee, The Right Brush, Snack Aisle, The Wheelchair Recycler, Cakes for Occasion, Bum Boosa®, and Mmofra Trom.[4] Additionally, as part

---

4. https://highereducationdevelopment.wordpress.com/models/ghana_project/

of my time at Bentley, I have guided students through directed studies, service learning and acted as a First Year Advisor. I am a huge proponent of the praxis approach and try to keep a paperless classroom. As you can see, for so many years, this has been such a passion of mine.

When you work at a University, there is a lot of autonomy. You work from home in the summer, trying to get your syllabus, your book selection, and your assignments planned out. Then when it is time to teach, you show up for your office hours an hour before your class; at the designated time, you then teach your class, and then you pack up and go home. It is a lonely job. After teaching at Bentley University, I can say that I really don't know any of my colleagues on a personal level. We just say "hi" if we happen to see each other in the hallway. It is like a barren desert, where I was not allowed to grow personally or collaboratively. I was starting to become stagnant.

I have always had a lot of energy, drive, and motivation. It is always in me, rumbling and grumbling in my solar plexus, and I wait until it boils over and bursts forth. Only then I can start the process of working on the next thing I am drawn to do. I think it is both innate and learned. I derive great pleasure from action and movement. So when COVID hit, I started to create.

According to the Urdu[5] dictionary, the definition of rebirth is "the action of reappearing or starting to flourish after a decline; revival, and revitalization; the process of being reincarnated or born again," just like the Phoenix rising from the ashes. I decided to apply this definition of rebirth to businesses. During COVID, the international business playing field was leveled and equalized. Many businesses closed, and thousands lost their jobs due to the pandemic. Some bemoaned the fact that business had been awful and that the economy would never recover. But there were others

---

5. Retrieved on December 13th, 2022, from: http://www.theurdudictionary.com/default.asp?word=rebirth&lang=en

who seized the opportunity to pivot: they changed their operations, learned recent technologies, welcomed remote learning and working, and they prospered. I saw this as the time to emerge, experience decline, and re-flourish to transform ideas, opportunities, and businesses into something that has great possibilities. So I started two new businesses and joined three others!

The first was a turnaround company that would help businesses be prepared for a sustainable future. This company was started with the help of Ray Chehata, former CEO of Hitachi Security Systems, and Jean-Louis Lam, founder and CEO of Cyber Exec. We offered packages on C-level coaching, 360° company-wide assessments, immediate solutions, operational excellence restart advice, talent acquisition, sales lead generation, legal, cyber resilience, compliance, and brand repositioning, to name some of the services. This company was very short-lived, however, as one of the primary partners got sick and couldn't fulfill their obligations, and therefore there was a failure to launch this business at its full capacity.

The second business I created was The Business Success Institute (BSI). BSI was developed as an integrated approach to business. While profits normally drive the majority of business endeavors, people ultimately are at the core of the business. Too often, the focus is on the bottom line of a company and not the people within these organizations. The Business Success Institute focuses on a heart-centered approach to individuals' needs within businesses, and by applying non-traditional business tools, techniques, and methods, BSI helps propel them to the next level of success, whatever that looks like to them. Using this heart-centered approach to business, I was able to co-lead a retreat and help facilitate workshops at a property that I invested in, located near Nicoya, Costa Rica, one of the five Blue Zones in the world. Incidentally, scientists, demographers, and anthropologists have studied Blue Zones as having the longest-living people on Earth.[6]

Additionally, during this time, I was briefly employed (1 ½ years) and accepted a full-time position as Vice President of Knowledge and Communications at US Capital Global, a private investment banking firm headquartered in San Francisco, CA. I specialized in capital market research and oversaw client originations, communications, and publications. I also helped businesses with due diligence to secure capital, from start-ups to established organizations.

The last two companies that I worked part-time at were Rodan + Fields,[7] an international skincare company, and Isagenix,[8] a plant-based health product company, both multi-level marketing companies. I made all my investment money back from R&F plus a little bit more, but with Isagenix, the selling team never came to fruition. Overall, I did not suffer finding work during the pandemic. In fact, I had my best year ever.

It took me a long time to tell my story and be proud and empowered about what I have accomplished in my life. From riches to rags, living in poverty made me realize that I was a thinker, smart, a strategist and that I loved to talk! Like most young girls, I didn't know what I wanted to be when I grew up. I just knew that I had limited career opportunities based on what my guidance counselor told me. A nurse, a teacher, a nutritionist. But I learned early on that education, no matter what I studied or whether it was at a University, broadened my sense of infinite possibilities and the likelihood that I could do anything and become anyone I wanted to be. This tenacity for learning, educating, and achieving drives what I do. Fast forward 40 years to where I am now:

---

6. Buettner, D., & Skemp, S. (2016). Blue Zones: Lesson lived from the world's longest lived. *American Journal of Lifestyle Medicine, 10*(5): 318–321. https://www.ncbi.nlm.nih.gov/pmc/articles/PMC6125071/
7. https://www.rodanandfields.com/en-us/
8. https://www.isagenix.com/en-us

An independent woman with five college degrees, including a Doctorate in Leadership with an emphasis in Organizational Behavior; along with a postdoctoral 3-year professional certificate from Harvard Extension School in Corporate Sustainability and Innovation.

25+ years as a Professor in Higher Education, including international lecturing, teaching management, marketing, and communication courses.

Owner of Roberta Pellant Consulting- helping leaders with strategy planning in management, marketing, and other unique projects. Certified professional development trainer, executive leadership coach, and motivational speaker.

Founder of The Business Success Institute- looking to transform leaders one business at a time. BSI was developed as a holistic approach to business, using a macro-driven team approach offering mini-MBA programs, energy coaching, RIM sessions, leadership workshops, Reiki healing, public speaking coaching, weekend, and week-long retreats.

Former Vice President of Knowledge and Communications at US Capital Global, an investment banking firm helping businesses with due diligence and developing certified business plans to secure capital, from start-ups to established organizations. I also oversaw capital market research, client origination communications, and publications.

Former Owner and Vice President of Organizational Development of Bum Boosa Bamboo Products® product launch, distribution, marketing, and entrepreneurship expertise.

I am a #1 International Bestselling Author, a TEDx speaker, educator, certified leadership coach and trainer with a vast global network of C-level executives across multiple industries in life. I have been featured on ABC Chronicle, in Wall Street Select, Yahoo! Finance, Market Watch, and International Business and am considered a top business financial success expert across all industries while helping leaders and businesses embrace failure to rise to the next level of their success.

If you asked that young girl where she would be today,

she could not have imagined. I wrote this section not only as the last healing piece of embarrassment, shame, anger, sadness, and pain for that young 12-year-old girl but also as concrete evidence to any woman (or man) that you are not a product of your circumstances. You can do anything you want to do. For many years, I wanted someone to come save me- a prince in shining armor, a Plan B fall back option, someone to help – of that deep-rooted fear of not having a roof over my head, food on the table, or being able to provide and take care of myself. Or just even the best things I knew I wanted in life.

—*Excerpted from Women Who Empower, 2020*

As you can see, I don't do anything halfway. There is no gray area, no neutral zone when it comes to my ambition. It surprised me to read somewhere that many women overachievers had family members that were not appreciative of their gifts, so they kept striving for bigger and better things so that they would be seen, appreciated, or accepted by them. Trying to prove one's worth is a vicious cycle that few get out of. I also fought so extremely hard to achieve all these things by myself, but I saw on Facebook recently that being extremely independent and busy is a sign of trauma. Not being able to ask for help most likely means that you are not trusting of other people, whether they have let you down or failed to help, so you would rather do it yourself. Wow.

I became unhealthily driven. I became obsessed with achieving my goals, making money. Greedy, if you will. I was working 3.5 jobs at one point in 2020, working seven days a week, never taking a day off. I was chasing dollars to feed my ego, which in turn I would use to buy expensive items as I was conditioned to do, $10,000 on *one* Chanel bag, $700 on a pair of Louis Vuitton shoes, over $150,000 on diamond jewelry, a $30,000 solid gold Rolex, not to mention other clothing items, that I just had to have. I don't say this to brag but to show you how crazy the ego can be! Every time I purchased a new item, I showed it off for a few days or weeks and then regaled it back into a box in my closet or under the bed. The vicious cycle that started in my marriage would continue to surface. The thrill of the chase was quickly over once I got what I wanted until the next time. I was unbalanced, with the Divine masculine dominating and my Divine feminine Being almost non-existent. I was very comfortable with this inequality as I was never taught or rarely used the Divine feminine energy. I thought it was a form of weakness.

By stepping into my Divine feminine more fully, I was able to readjust my motives and actions for working, and instead of coming from an ego-driven appetite, I became more in alignment with meaning fulfilled with purpose for the Universe. With this Spiritual marriage of both the feminine and masculine balanced within me, I was able to achieve a more peaceful nature of just *Being*. I gave up my investment banking job without a fight in 2021 and made the decision at the end of 2022 that I would step back from teaching, sell my ownership share in Costa Rica, and in early 2023, found myself no longer working 80+ hours a week. I was being guided to step back to honor what felt right for me.

Brothers

> "Once a brother, always a brother, no matter the distance, no matter the difference, and no matter the issue."
>
> —*Byron Pulsifer*

I waited until now to talk about my relationship with my three brothers because I did not grow up with them per se. We really didn't have a strong connection or relationship to speak of when I was younger. It was only when our father died on December 12th, 2006, that we started to re-establish the relationships, and we became the closest of friends.

The oldest twin, Jim, has struggled with drinking since he

was around 13 years old. He never married or had children. While I was away at college and during my marriage, his life was a series of Driving While Intoxicated (D.W.I.) violations, charges, and sentences. I believe there were at least six, making the last one a felony, and he served around a year's time in a state prison for the last one.

For years, I did not talk to him, as he was always drunk, slurring his words, and it triggered me. It was so much easier to ignore him and the situation. It was too painful. Out of sight, out of mind. Sticking my head in the sand. No compassion or empathy for my own flesh and blood. Not my problem. Thinking it could have been me; after all, we share the same DNA. I was so overcome by guilt, shame, and embarrassment of him and me. I'm a coward. I likened his and my life to a movie called *Grey Gardens*. But through my healing process, I realized that he had choices as well and that it was his life. Nevertheless, I will always support and love him deeply.

I am very thankful that he never hurt himself, another person, or an animal and that his license has been suspended and he won't be able to get it back. I am saddened that he still struggles with this disease, despite numerous attempts in rehab and the tremendous toll it has taken on his body and liver. When mortality is brought into question, I decided that I wanted to get back to a sibling friendship because when he is not drinking, he is loving, kind, gentle, hilarious, and has the best long-term memory out of all of us. So not long ago, I wrote him a very heartfelt letter asking him questions that I had answers to and establishing some boundaries. I told him that I would love to talk to him, but only if he wasn't drinking. The result of me saying that and him respecting those wishes have resulted in some great deep-hearted conversations, which I hope to continue for the rest of our lives. Knowing he is safe, and taken care of, living in a house on my parents' property that my younger brother Mike built for him, allows me peace.

Jon, the youngest twin, and I had some major brouhahas

growing up. He is stubborn like I am, and when I was younger, I knew just how to provoke him and push every button. Jon married, had two children around my children's age, Shelby and Kyle, and then divorced. He works hard during the day and then works even harder at night as a mechanic. We both started talking about problems with ex-spouses, children, life in general, and bonding, as only one can do with another who has gone through similar experiences. We talk all the time, and I found that we can have a lot of fun when we are together. He is one of my best friends.

    Mike is 11 years younger than me. He bought a house at 18 that abuts my parents' property, working delivering gas during the day and pulling double duty as the town's Fire Chief in Gordon, WI. Since he lives in the same town, nearly 100% of the caretaking responsibilities for my father and Jim fell on him, both timewise and, in the case of Jim, financially. Yes, once again, I felt guilt, shame, and embarrassment that I wasn't doing my part with them, but I had a great conversation with Mike, and there was no resentment there. Jon is around 2.5 hours away in Aitkin, MN and helps out whenever he is in town, dropping everything when there is an emergency, but Mikey had to grow up the fastest as he was only 17 years old when my mom died. He never married, had no children, and he really has been the strongest pillar of strength in our family. He is so rational, stable, a man of little words, and so dang goofy (he would say the same about me) that I adore and love him to pieces. We also talk and text all the time. I can't wait until the next time I see them all.

Dating After Divorce

> "A bad relationship can do that; can make you doubt everything good you ever felt about yourself."
>
> —*Dionne Warwick*

> "What we fear of doing most is usually what we most need to do."
>
> —*Ralph Emerson*

Because I had lost fragments of Soul, I also tended to ignore red flags in relationships. Ironically, because I listened to everyone else in my life, I ignored what Soul was telling me. I didn't listen either to what the Universe was trying to tell me. I ignored the signs so many times. I lost my internal alarm system to flee. If someone were overly attentive and flattering to me, I would take the bait, time and time again. What that meant was that Spirit would die off a little bit more, as I would get sucked into the vortex of *their* life, like a tourist visiting. These relationships, while at first appearance seemed to be good for me, nurturing, deep, and potentially long-lasting, turned out not to be sustainable. I would overlook my instincts to run away after something bad happened and put my blinders on once again. I never thought that I wanted to change the person I was with, I was just the perpetually happy, hopeful person that I could make this work, and if it wasn't working, I would put my head in the sand. I was so hungry for connection, and Soul was so starved that I would get caught up in relationships for years, even though only months into the relationship, my intuition told me to run. I embody the term "head over heels in love" fully. When I fall, I fall fast. I throw caution to the wind, and when this happens, the fire cannot be put out. When a person feels starved, they will take any offering they can get in order to feel nourished. In this case, I was feeding myself poison.

I failed to see the betrayals to Spirit in every single one of these relationships. Betrayals of broken promises, false truths, masks of who they wanted me to see, not standing up for me or us, betrayals of not helping me when I was sick, pulling me and pushing me to walk on their path, the "I need you" and "I will make you happy" and the biggest one: betrayal of the hope of a future together.

It will come as no surprise to anyone, but the shocking first couple of pages, titled, *Flashback- Counting,* were written during the time that I was in a long-term relationship with S, going through a long, drawn-out, arduous divorce. I was not quite divorced from J. when I met S. at a party. I was not at all interested in dating anyone; however, he managed to charm me and put little pressure on me to date. I felt I could take my time with this casual friendship, and let it see where it would take us. Quickly the love-bombing and grand romantic gestures started, followed by the silences and the tiffs over something stupid, and then the sheepish re-connecting from him. I should have walked away a few months into the relationship when I found out that he had returned a kiss from someone else at a bar. A major red flag once again, but I chose to ignore it and shove it away.

In this relationship, much more so than any of the others, I felt like a child. Maybe this was because S. resembled my father physically, very tall and handsome, with mitts for hands and a gruff presence. I became so attached to him, needing his approval, his love, and his admiration because I was missing that after my father died. S. told me to be nice to everyone, to not talk as much about myself or my children, to act a certain way, a carbon copy of all the other country club women on the Cape with their white jeans, wedge heels, and designer sunglasses. I had no interest; I had been there and done that. But I tried to fit in. Oftentimes he would ask me, "Are you a good girl?" just to verify I was toeing the line. I not only acquiesced to him but to others as well. I felt that I was not allowed to dream big or yearn for self-fulfillment and what Soul wanted. I was supposed to follow along with what everybody else was doing and what was considered acceptable and normal. And I conceded. Voluntarily, once again, I stepped headfirst into another person's orbit, their philosophies, their way of life, not thinking about what I truly desired, and within a short period of time, became incredibly sad, and yearned to be free, daydreamed about finding someone else to rescue me. My thoughts included finding someone else that was better, walking away from the relationship because this was too hard, and at times hating the person I was with. And while I am not proud of this, just like in my marriage, I did this several times. Spirit was broken, and I became compliant. There was no support, no encouragement, no being fed on a Soul level. I stopped seeking, learning, being and was robotic in every way. It was like I was walking around in a sleep or fugue-like state.

I was unsatisfied. I still had deep, hidden, unhealed trauma, not only mine but trauma passed down through the generations. There was a distinct duality in my relationship with myself and with others. Soul authenticity was not matching behaviors, and behaviors were not matching words. For me, I know that the shame that cut away a piece of Soul inhibited me from taking actions out of fear.

For 15 years of my life, as well as with my 20-year marriage before that, the meaningful life I knew I was meant to have was seduced away from me by settling, staying in my comfort zone, and wanting to be loved. I needed to do something drastically different, and that would be to go back to inner Spirit and reestablish the relationship with Self. I needed to sit in the discomfort of being alone, without a man, and learn to love myself again. I knew I had some Spirit left; for it never dies. It was in me when I challenged every rule my parents laid down for me. It was in me when I pursued my education, my dreams, when filing for divorce, or leaving a relationship. I just had to remember where it was in me. Rebirth and remerge.

This would be the toughest and most painful battle I have ever fought; fighting internal demons. Deep in the inner recesses of my nature, just like deep in the ground, is where the richest soil is. If you dig deep enough and plant a seed, the most beautiful flower will emerge, just like the lotus breaking through the mud. This was so significant to me to release that at 50 years old, I got a small, not opened lotus flower tattoo on my foot, a visual reminder without the struggle, there would be no lotus. Not opened because the blooming process was just beginning, and I was far from full bloom enlightenment.

I carried deep trauma, PTSD-like anxiety and was numb and exhausted. I *knew* I needed an expectation of fidelity and a real commitment to feel safe. I was rock bottom emotionally, but I was not ruined. I finally knew enough was enough, and I was determined to do my shadow work around inner Soul, rebuilding myself, and creating healthy boundaries in the process. I would regain my confidence, self-worth, and perception in order to be reborn. I was freeing myself from the addiction of having a partner, and I was going to take *my* life back. But I wasn't going to try to do it alone as a victim this time. I would rally my tribe, my chosen family around me.

Relationships are meant not to complete Self but to complement Self. I was searching for relationships that were congruent with Soul needs, One that I wanted to co-create in this lifetime. I wanted One who was well-integrated, who had done the hard work internally, and was full of Self-Love. A Lightworker, Starseed, i.e., One who had expanded awareness. While I was seeking this externally, I discovered it was not with another, but the relationship I sought was with this human body in relationship with inner Soul.

It was time. Time to return back to where I came from. It was time to rise up from the ashes. My life as I knew it was over; and that was a good thing. I would choose to repair what was injured. I knew it was required to take off my blinders and rose-colored glasses and look deeper into Soul. It was imperative for healing to feel into my intuition, stay still, and not run away. It was also necessary for me to set my own firm boundaries. It was absolutely essential to rid my human body of the shame and any other trauma I was carrying. And so began initiation in earnest to re-merge with Soul.

PART III:
Seeking Oneness with Soul

The Spring: Picking Up the Pieces

"Intuition will tell the thinking mind where to look next."

—Jonas Salk

I decided to start journeying inward when I got divorced. I was desperately gasping for anything that would take the pain away to help me heal. As you can imagine, I did not have a supportive partner on my quest. This is not any fault of his. He just didn't understand it, judged it, as many times it was considered out there and not mainstream. I was living in the past while wanting to live in the future. What I need to do is be present in the here and now.

I had been sleepwalking through my messy life with blinders and rose-colored glasses on. Up until now, I had been serving the needs of Others: mother, wife, teacher, servant. For years, without knowing it, I was seeking liberation and rebirth of Soul. By sheer will and flow to return back to Spirit, without full support from ordinary society, I write this next chapter of my life. These are most of the interventions, methods, counseling, books, seminars, and religions that I sought out to kickstart the process of deep healing.

The next sections are esoteric at best. Understood by few, and while I have been studying and practicing these subjects for several years, I still find myself unable at times to fully grasp them as well. But I will attempt to explain them the best I can, bridging the rational brain and physical body with unexplained miracles and the woo-woo beliefs of Spirit.

My Spiritual Quest and Deepak Chopra

> "You're a Spiritual being having a human experience. You're not a human being having a Spiritual experience."
>
> —*Deepak Chopra*

Like most adults, when going through tough times in life, I turned to traditional talk therapy. This was the only thing that I thought was available to me at the time, it was widely accepted, and mainstream, and my health insurance covered most of the costs. From around the ages of 30-44 years old (a few years when I was younger and older as well), I sought out different therapists, some by myself, some with my significant others. Most of the time, it would just be me venting to the counselor with little feedback or deep insight as to the issue at hand. I would also, most of the time, go away feeling unsatisfied with the process and that nothing had been resolved.

I don't exactly recall how I discovered Deepak Chopra,[1] but I signed up for a retreat In Carlsbad, CA, at the Chopra Center[2] and was mesmerized by the workshops on Ayurvedic practices, eating vegetarian, meditation practices, and quantum physics talks. This was the first time that I was exposed to Eastern philosophy and Transcendental Meditation. I had my Vedic (based on the Vedas, Hindu Scriptures) astrological birth chart done (sun, moon, stars, and planet placement) and was given my own mantra that mimicked the sound of the Universe at the exact moment I was born. I learned about chakra balancing, clearing each one with a different Sanskrit[3] sound and envisioning the corresponding color associated with the seven chakras throughout the body, releasing any blockages. I learned how to go through the

---

1. https://www.deepakchopra.com/
2. As of January 31, 2023, the Chopra Center in this location has closed.
3. \\Sanskrit is the ancient language of India and Hinduism. Retrieved on February 5th, 2023, from: https://www.yogapedia.com/definition/4959/sanskrit

movement of flow by practicing the 12 positions of Sun Salutation yoga while reciting the corresponding Sanskrit mantras with each pose. I started doing dry brushing and abhyanga massage on myself, using nasya oils in my nose and ears, Basti enemas, practicing different pranayama breathwork techniques, swishing my mouth with coconut oil or pulling as it is sometimes referred to, and tongue scraping to detox, along other Ayurvedic customs of purification. I balanced my dosha (the genetic constitution of my body), which was mainly Pitta (energetic, solid, stable), but could easily swing to Vata (fast, anxious, airiness), or Kapha (slow, dense, heavy), depending on the season. These practices, for the first time in my life, helped quell my anxiety and quiet my mind. I met Deepak after he spoke at the Center, talking to him about Boston and my time at Harvard University while in his office, and I remember thinking he reminded me of a wise owl that was always the observer in present moment awareness. I became enamored by him for years, signing up for workshops, even embarking on a 10-day silent retreat with no communication with anyone, no eye contact, no books, tv, or contact by cell phone, only my journal, nature, and what seemed like endless hours of meditation per day. When I came out of that particular retreat, colors seemed more vibrant, people seemed more loving, sounds were crisper, and I flew home happy and re-centered. Deepak and I would continue to correspond via email in between retreats, and I was privy to some of his upcoming ideas for new business ventures. I was able to meet many of his guest speakers, such as Dr. Mark Hyman[4] (*The Blood Sugar Solution*), nutritionist Kimberly Snyder[5] (*Radical Beauty*), and Gabby Bernstein[6] (*Spirit Junkie*).

    My Spiritual journey, restlessness to find something, and the quest for alternative methods of healing were in full swing during this time. Through him, I was also introduced to the

---

4. https://drhyman.com/
5. https://mysolluna.com/
6. https://gabbybernstein.com/

works of Caroline Myss[7] (*Scared Contracts)*, casting my chart of origin and studying archetypes. I learned EFT[8] (emotional freedom technique) or tapping, visualization, and manifesting, different Hindu, and Buddhist practices, along with daily affirmation practices said aloud. I read anything I could get my hands on that Deepak (*The Seven Spiritual Laws of Success; The Book of Secrets)* recommended, including most, if not all, of his books. Books by Marianne Williamson[9] (*A Return to Love: Reflections on the Principles of A Course in Miracles),* Jack Canfield[10] (Co-Founder of *Chicken Soup for the Soul* books; *The Success Principles*), Brené Brown[11] *(Daring Greatly; Rising Strong)*, Dr. Wayne Dyer[12] *(The Power of Awakening: Mindfulness Practices and Spiritual Tools to Transform Your Life)*, and Dr. Andrew Weil[13] *(Spontaneous Healing)*, who smiled at me one day while sitting outside on a bench at the Chopra Center. I learned about Mary Morrissey[14] and took her 3-day online Dream Builder course. My thirst for knowledge for knowing and improving myself, my mind, and my body were at an all-time high. I would take copious notes and be so open-minded, only to find myself searching for the next best thing.

 I dabbled in traditional Western astrology and still do, having my natal/birth and my moon charts plotted. I am a Sun Cancer, which is a cardinal water sign, ruled by the moon, which was waning at the time of my birth, and Aquarius rising. This means I am emotional and sensitive; I have an intuitive understanding of energy around me, and I like

---

7. https://www.myss.com/
8. A how to guide on EFT can be found on this site.
Littlefield, M. (Medical Reviewer). (2022). Emotional Freedom Technique (EFT). Retrieved on February 5th, 2023, from: https://www.nyp.org/healthlibrary/articles/emotional-freedom-technique-eft
9. https://marianne.com/
10. https://jackcanfield.com/
11. https://brenebrown.com/
12. https://www.drwaynedyer.com/
13. https://www.drweil.com/
14. https://www.marymorrissey.com/

innovative ideas and concepts.[15] My moon is in Aries, which means I am high-spirited and courageous. I am fiery, impulsive and have a strong drive to accomplish any goal I might have. I am passionate, fully loving, and gifted with an impressive way with words.[16] For a free birth chart from Astrolabe, see the link below.[17] Moon reading also will provide a free moon chart.[18] For both readings, please make sure you know the exact time of your birth and the city in which you were born.

I took webinars in Astro-numerology to discover my divine codes. My birth date number and life purpose number are a five: meaning I am intelligent, humorous, full of adventure, and a seeker of greater existence, looking for the deeper meaning of life.[19] My destiny number is six, meaning I am a good storyteller, homey, romantic, considerate, and love to travel.[20] Lastly, my wealthy name number is eight, which means I am forceful, high achieving, Spiritually conscious, and able to achieve more wealth than most, making me successful in business.[21]

I made vision boards, worked through the steps and *Success Principles™*, and wrote out my childhood poverty trauma in a chapter in *Women Who Empower*[22], which by the way, became a #1 and #2 International bestselling book in 5 countries. I met with Linda Howe[23] to have my Akashic

---

15. Retrieved on January 1st, 2008, from: https://alabe.com/
16. Retrieved on July 2nd, 2022, from: https://www.moonreading.com/
17. https://alabe.com/freechart/
18. https://www.moonreading.com/
19. Beringer, B. (2022). The life path 5 meaning, explained. Retrieved on February 5th, 2023, from: https://www.bustle.com/life/life-path-5-in-numerology-meaning
20. Retrieved on February 5th, 2023, from: https://www.astrogle.com/numerology/destiny-number-or-fadic-number-6.html
21. Walmsley, J. (2010). Numerology-The vibration and meaning of numbers. Name number 8. 8 Positive Attributes. Retrieved on February 5th, 2023, from: http://numerology-thenumbersandtheirmeanings.blogspot.com/2010/10/name-number-8.html
22. https://www.amazon.com/Women-Who-Empower-Stories-Heart/dp/195272533X
23. https://lindahowe.com/

(Book of Life) records read. I paid for mediums and tarot card readings. I have participated in ghost tours, learning more about the local people that have walked before me.[24] I briefly sought out and yearned to become initiated into Hinduism; chanting *"Hare Krishna, Hare Rama..."* over and over again while holding a Japa mala, attending festivals, and singing kirtan in Ashrams. I tried everything known to me to help and heal myself in this physical world, constantly learning and searching, searching, searching, never finding the answer. Trying without words to get back to Soul alignment, not only to find my innocent child again but also to seek out past ancestral experiences to heal as well.

    I was scattered. I was searching for my tribe, trying to feel like I truly belonged to something. I was on the path that felt right, but I was met with many twists and turns, and I had to make conscious decisions. Sometimes I would backtrack to get on a better path for me. Other times I would just end up in a circle, determined to find me again. One thing I have never wavered on is my ability to keep going. To never give up on searching for where I belong. The trip back to who I once was long ago. The perseverance and the tenacity were deeply rooted inside of me, just knowing to keep looking. No matter what the obstacle, I knew it in Soul to not give up on this quest because around every dangerous curve, no matter how dark or scary or how long it would take me miles, I knew there would be a beautiful river, a rainbow in the sky, a full moon as a reminder to keep going on this Spiritual journey. While all these teachings and practices worked for me, I still had failed to integrate my ego self with Soul to become One. The Soul is the birther of the Spirit. The Spirit is the essence of the Soul.

    I eventually realized I was searching externally and was looking outward toward others and that the answer had always been inside of me. Finding it again would be in the 5th

---

24. https://www.blockislandghosttours.com/ Please check the website for current offerings.

and 6th-dimensional metaphysical world, the space between the atoms. I just had to be extremely still and listen. I just needed to stop wandering in a state of searching due to Spirit being parched and return back to Soul, back to the Divine child I once was. There was no talking myself out of this, no jumping into the distractions of life. Instinct and innerness would take priority. But how to attain this, and get to this place?

I've never really done the demanding work on myself. I have blamed my parents and the product of my circumstances, my relationships, my drinking, and my children for nearly everything that has gone wrong in my life. Even though I have searched to the ends of the Earth to figure out what was wrong with me, when I couldn't put a label on it, I pointed the finger at something else until I met Mother Ayahuasca.

Finding Soul and Merging Back: Ayahuasca

> "You have to grow from inside out. None can teach you; none can make you Spiritual. There is no other teacher but your own soul."
>
> —*Swami Vivekananda*

I want readers to understand that I did much scientific research and vetting of not only the medicines I am writing about but also the Spiritual healers leading the ceremonies. Most, if not all, have a deep indigenous lineage with these medicines spanning hundreds of years. Others have studied for many years learning from these *Grandfathers*. I have only used these medicines in their pure, naturally occurring, non-synthetically derived form. My undertaking of these alternative forms of healing was done solely for Spiritual exploration, not as a way to elicit a drug-induced high, and I reverently participated in these rituals, being respectful of the cultural beliefs associated with them. In an article I read by Dr. Weil and his colleague, Dr. Davis (1994) they stated that the pharmacologically active compounds found in these plants or animals are determined by a *cultural* dosage, as to if they become a hallucinogen, medicine, or poison (drug).[25] All medicines come with side effects, some unpleasant at times. That really resonated with me, and I humbly ask you to read with an open mind and with regard to the cultural history of these powerful medicines.

Ayahuasca, Aya, ceremonial tea, or Yagé as it can be called, has gained a following with many celebrities who have come out publicly about their experience. Most recently with Green Bay Packer Quarterback Aaron Rodgers[26] and Prince Harry[27] *(Spare)*. "Aya" translates to Spirit or Soul and "huasca" is vine, so it means "Vine of the Spirit." The main psychoactive or hallucinogenic ingredient in Ayahuasca is N, N-dimethyltryptamine (DMT), and unlike some other drugs, hallucinogenic ones tend not to be highly addictive or abused.[28] It should be noted that since Ayahuasca contains DMT, which is a Schedule I substance in the United States, it is illegal to possess.[29] Research literature suggests that the therapeutic benefits of Ayahuasca may include helping with and overcoming addictions, improved mood, decreased anxiety and depression, as well as being beneficial to those suffering

---

25. Weil, A. and Davis, W. (1994). Bufo alvarius: A potent hallucinogen of animal origin. *Journal of Ethnopharmacology, 41*(1–2): 1–8. https://www.sciencedirect.com/science/article/abs/pii/0378874194900515
26. Stump, S. (2022). Aaron Rodgers explains how ayahuasca changed his life. Retrieved on February 8th, 2023, from: https://www.today.com/news/sports/aaron-rodgers-ayahuasca-experiences-healing-rcna42205
27. Wales, H. (2023). *Spare*. (p. 255). Random House.
28. Facts and info on ayahuasca (DMT). (2022). Retrieved on September 20th, 2022, from: https://americanaddictioncenters.org/psychedelics/ayahuasca
29. United States Department of Justice Drug Enforcement Administration Controlled Substances www.deadiversion.usdoj.gov/schedules/orangebook/c_cs_alpha.pdf Retrieved August 3rd, 2021, from: https://www.deadiversion.usdoj.gov/schedules/

from post-traumatic stress disorder (PTSD).[30] Contraindications, other than purging, are generally seen in individuals with underlying psychiatric disorders and health conditions, medication interactions, older age, and taking Ayahuasca in a non-supervised environment.[31]

I first heard about Aya years ago from Deepak's use of it in Peru, but I never gave it much thought. Aya is a plant from South America, cultivated and brewed from the vine of one tree and mixed with the leaves of a different shrub. Yagé is a Shamanic ceremonial medicine that the Taitas (Columbian Indigenous healer, or Papa) believe can heal anything. As clinical studies listed above: drug and substance addiction, PTSD, anxiety, and depression. The Taitas also believe Aya heals sexual, physical, and emotional traumas, any physical ailments, or diseases, along with deep-rooted fears and triggers passed down from generations. It is an intense, mysterious, miraculous, altered, conscious-less, psychedelic experience, allowing the mind to step away from the ego and experience a different reality to help individuals embrace reality differently. Aya does not allow the ego to control the experience. The more people fight to let go of their ego, the harder the journey becomes, and healing doesn't happen. Just when someone "plans" to have one type of ceremony, the opposite thing happens. There must be openness, welcoming, and curiosity to the adventure, allowing oneself to be carried throughout the journey, not the one driving to the destination, but instead being one with the flow. The words Ayahuasca and Yagé are capitalized in this book in deference to the Taitas and their cultures and the belief in the Spiritual properties of the medicine.

---

30. Nižnanský et al. (2022). Ayahuasca as a decoction applied to human: Analytical methods, pharmacology, and potential toxic effects. *Journal of Clinical Medicine,* 11(4): 1–21. https://www.mdpi.com/2077-0383/11/4/1147

31. Bouso et al. (2022). Adverse effects of ayahuasca: Results from the global ayahuasca survey. *PLOS Glob Public Health*, 2(11): 1:25. https://journals.plos.org/globalpublichealth/article?id=10.1371/journal.pgph.0000438

I signed up for an Ayahuasca ceremony five minutes after I met my friend and, ultimately, Soul Sister, Cathleen. We were on a Zoom call for something else that we had both signed up for, and she mentioned how Aya had helped her heal through the loss and transition of her son, Logan. She had participated in her 1st ceremony earlier that year at Rythmia Life Advancement Center[32] in Costa Rica (CR), an all-inclusive, luxury, medically licensed Spiritual retreat space, and was heading back in the next four months. Cathleen asked me if I wanted to come and room with her, and as soon as I got off the call, I booked my spot. The only thing she said I needed to know before I went was to be open to hear the call to drink the medicine or tea and that for the nightly ceremonies, I should bring all-white clothes. White signifies purity and, in some cultures, the preparation for death (of the ego) and protection from negative energy. Additionally, a special *dieta* or diet of no meat, no alcohol or other drugs, low sodium, sugar, and fat was to be started two weeks prior to arrival to show motivation and dedication to the plant ceremonies and the corresponding beliefs of the Taitas. It is important to emphasize that individuals that use selective serotonin reuptake inhibitors (SSRIs) are not good patients for this type of medicine and will not be served in ceremony.

I watched some videos on Aya and did my research. I liked the fact that Rythmia had licensed physicians, paramedics, and nurses on staff and that they would do a full medical intake before allowing participants to partake in the medicine. I was to set my intention before arrival, meditating, journaling, and Being one with nature as much as I could. I remember one day taking my normal 30-minute walk and coming back into the driveway, noticing the white Birch tree in front of the house, and just hugging it for a few moments, thanking it. Much later, I learned that it was Mother Aya already working within me, preparing me for my healing. I was not fearful at all but rather excited and happy to be able

---

32. https://www.rythmia.com/

to have this trip planned in my future. I did not talk about it to many people, my brothers and S. and all, if not most of them, thought I had lost my mind.

It was December 2020, and we were right in the midst of the pandemic. I was so worried that this momentous opportunity would be canceled! But the Universe was working in my favor. All Costa Rica needed was added travel insurance, and Rythmia would require a negative COVID test before arrival upon the property. I met Cathleen in Miami, and once we landed in the CR, we were transported with a few others, including a well-known movie actor, from Liberia to Guanacaste, where the resort is situated. In the parking lot were tents with nurses who would give us another precautionary rapid COVID blood test before allowing us to remove our masks and step on the property. Once on the property, we had to stay for health reasons.

The first couple of days, temperatures were obtained at mealtimes, medicals were done, and preparation classes like breathwork, good questions to ask of yourself in ceremony, and history of plant medicine were taken. Tokens for the nightly ceremonies, massages, shot glasses to drink the "tea" from, and colon cleanses to help in the purification process were also handed out. Normally ceremonies at Rythmia are full, with around 100 people attending, but due to COVID, the week I went, there were only around 65 participants. It was a significant week; Taita Juanito, one of the most powerful, revered Spiritual leaders of the Ingano Pueblo tribe, descended from the Incas, and Siona Tribes, from Putumayo, Colombia, was the one in attendance. Taita Juan is the "founder of Finca Ambiwasi Healing Centre and has dedicated his life's mission to healing the world, helping anyone who comes to him, and giving back to his community."[33] I would be in ceremony for four nights, two with him. Before I had my first ceremony, I met one on one with Taita

---

33. Retrieved on February 2nd, 2023, from: https://magicfundamazon.com/about-us/

Juanito and told him about my intentions through his interpreter, Carlos. I also presented him with a piece of the birch bark that I had brought with me as a gift from nature. Taita Juanito is so powerful that once, when he walked into a classroom and turned the corner, my head snapped back when his energy met with mine.

I had to stop eating solid foods after 2 or 3 p.m. on each of the days I participated in ceremony. At around 6:30 p.m. I would walk into the maloca (covered long peaked structure) and choose a single bed. Each bed had a pillow, sheet, blanket, roll of toilet paper, and a big bucket (to catch the vomit) near it. While it is not encouraged to be next to a friend, family member, or significant other, as you might not experience your own healing journey due to the sounds or behaviors coming from them. Cathleen and I chose to be side by side with a Shaman that was helping on my side. Even after this first time I chose to have a Shaman helper next to me. With Cathleen always next to me, we can stay in our own lane, so to speak, and not interfere with each other's journeying. I meditated, journaled, reflected on my intentions, and did hapé to calm me down. More on the practice of hapé later.

The first two nights starting at 7:30 or 8 p.m., Shamans trained by a particular Taita will put their own blessing into the Aya. Music is played, lights dimmed, everyone is silent, and the 1st cup is called. Men form a line on one side, women on another. It is worth mentioning that no women on their moon (menstruating) would be allowed to join in the ceremony, as Shamans believe this is a powerful purification ritual in its own right. When it was my time to be served the Aya, the Shaman said a prayer, and before drinking, I whispered my intention into the cup. I drank it down with one gulp. It tastes a little bitter, is thick brown, and a bit sweet, something like dirty molasses or licorice. It sometimes has particles of twigs and leaves in it, which makes it hard to get down. I never minded the taste of it, but most people find it repulsive. After drinking, I walked back to my bed, sitting up for around 15–20 minutes, waiting for the medicine to take effect.

Ayahuasca whips your ass, literally and figuratively. She does not care about age, gender, education level, profession, or salary, and most everyone will experience a purging of some kind, whether that be throwing up, urinating, yawning, calling out, shaking, or having diarrhea, to help facilitate the healing process. There was no pomp and circumstance associated with the ceremonies I participated in, and in the end, the individuals had no sense of ego or embarrassment for what happened during the night. If participants allow openness and flow, they will receive healing and purification of the body.

In the first two ceremonies, I did not purge, no vomiting, no diarrhea. It was explained to me in the preparation classes that several things could happen while on the medicine. I could have a pinta (seeing visions or Sacred geometry patterns), body work, a surgery (where there might be pain felt and alien Beings feel like they are working on places of my body), or a death, a consulta (where there could be a conversation with someone or something that provides guidance, delivers a message, or answers a question), or have a nada (a deep sleep where nothing is seen, felt, or heard). Aya is associated with the form of a black snake, so it was explained that I might see that as well. It is quite common for people to experience death during this time, and most have a major fear of this. I had told myself that I would not be afraid, I would trust in the healing process. Interestingly, while I wasn't afraid to die metaphorically, I couldn't let unhealthy relationships die.

During my ceremonies, I learned to separate thought (intellect/rationalization) from feeling (intuition, knowing). I saw beautiful pintas, Sacred geometry, my ancestors dancing around a candle, and the most vibrant and beautiful indescribable colors. I heard lovely Angelic voices, who called my name, along with whispers of hope and Love. I felt such joy and unparalleled happiness.

But all the hard work happens on the dark side of the

journey. I remember Gerry, the owner of Rythmia, telling us, "If you see three doors on a journey, and two are bright and inviting, and one is dark and scary, open the dark one; this is where the answers and the healing lies." Going into the darkness yet remaining in Soul and using every part of my intuition led to great insights. Because I genuinely believed that the deepest work and healing from Aya came from this darkness, I chose to do the work. In this darkness, I learned to "see" very clearly. Clearer than I have ever seen before. Needing to ask the hard and right questions to be healed and transformed is crucial. *"Show me what I have become. Merge me back with my soul at all costs. Heal my heart."*[34] These questions were truly the key to remerging back to Soul. I needed to do the inner work and act on my own behalf for healing, and not follow anyone else's suggestions. I chose to pick the dark door versus the light-filled one when I saw it.

With Mother Aya, to be truly conscious on a Soul level, you must at times embrace the darkness through death. Sometimes it felt like literally dying; other times it was symbolic, with no pain associated with it. In one of my ceremonies I was asked by a black, terrifying snake (Mother Aya) to open my mouth. When I overcame the fear and welcomed her into me, suddenly, I was reborn as a small baby black snake in a dry riverbed calling out for my mother. Knowing that she was near, but also having the strength to be independent. I saw that I could become a dependent person, whether in relationships or friendships. Through this rebirth, I saw that I could be alone and thrive while always feeling the presence of Others. This death experience has happened several other times to me in other ceremonies, but the vision was always much different, with a different realization attached to it. Trust was extremely important at this point in Spiritual visioning because what I have learned through these experi-

---

34. Taken from a preparatory classroom at Rythmia Life Advancement Center. (2020). https://www.rythmia.com/

ences is that we never die forever; it is just my ego that dies or my physical body, but never Soul.

The second two nights of Yagé, I purged, and while I am a dainty, quiet vomiter, as soon as I got up on all fours to purge, as I was taught to do, my human Angel, Luis, was right there alongside me, whispering encouragement in my ear, telling me to let it go, and handing me a piece of tissue when I was done. We learned that after purging to look into our bucket and see what it represents. The first time I saw a bunch of cigarettes flowing around in mud. I was purging for me and any issues I had with my mother, who chained smoked Salem menthol 100s. The second time I purged, I saw the world. I knew then I was purging for humanity. One other time, after drinking Yagé, I sat straight up and purged. It was effortless, and I had no problem with it. I was head-to-head with another person in ceremony that had a really tough time all night long with vomiting. I recognized that this purge was not mine to observe in the bucket, but that I was being called to help her purge.

I love the taste of Yagé. It tastes sweeter than Aya. My intention with the Taita was to see Nirvana, and Yagé did not disappoint. I went into the nothingness and saw the spaciousness, quiet of the Universe. I went to the space of creation and the Source. It only took one cup of Yagé. On one of my journeys, I saw a big white book, and the pages were turning. It reminded me of someone changing the channels on a television very quickly. I was able to see glimpses and frames of people and places, and then it stopped. When I asked Taita to help me explain what I saw, he told me I saw the Book of Life.

Not everyone has such blissful experiences. If someone is having a hard time with the purging or the medicine, Shamans will come to their bed to bless them with chanting, shaking rattles, fanning them with feathers and the smoke of copal resin burning in metal buckets, or tapping them using stinging nettle palms and agua de Florida water that they put in their mouth and spray out on them to help with the process and clear the heavy energy. This is also done to everyone at sunrise when people sit lotus style (crossed-legged), palms up, in healing circle limpiezas (cleansing), getting cleared and blessed by all of the Shamans individually. When healing, they use a whooshing breath that sounds like 'ushtau' which means the breath of life, the point of origin, the universal Source sound when Soul comes into the world. Individuals are encouraged to strip down to expose as much skin as possible. Men are shirtless, and women are down to a tank top. Each Shaman will chant and pray over and in front of you for several minutes, with a female helper behind you, singing and laying their hands on you. At the end of this ritual, they will rub beautifully fragrant sweet lotions on all exposed parts of your skin. It is one of my most favorite parts of the ceremony, after a hard night's work.

The reintegration of the *Soul* is embodied by the symbol of the Ankh, ☥, an Egyptian hieroglyph used to represent the word life. Imagine a Venn diagram with two circles intersecting in the middle. The ego, one circle, is rational, common sense. The other circle is the Soul in a mystical, intuitive sense. It is in the space in the center where the circles meet or merge. This space is represented in the center of the Ankh and the Soul, which has no beginning and no end. I am, I feel, I will, I love, I speak, I see, and I know that my Light and Love are projecting outwardly into this world. Each time I became One with Aya, I re-merged with Soul, I became stronger, forging the ego to stay centered in Soul.

While I started the ceremony in all-white pristine clothing and traveled all night, sometimes I awoke at sunrise, covered and stained animalistically with splashes of vomit and Aya from my cup. Others, who did not see a need for a diaper, stood up with their blankets wrapped around their waist as a telltale sign that they let go, releasing from the other end. Participants lose all sense of the ego, for Aya strips away any shame or fear associated with appearances. I am One. One with each other, One with nature, One with the Universe. I am not of the body; I have a body. I ascend or descend many times into the primal nature of the Universe, learning new ways to experience love, learning to overcome fear, and learning to just be. My realities change. Things that used to motivate and excite me no longer hold me hostage. Relationships that I thought were once great now seem stale in comparison. When I go back home and re-integrate into society, everything seems dull and depressing. I miss the Love of my Tribe in ceremony.

Cathleen was hearing the call of another Aya ceremony, and ended up staying one more week, and as much as I wanted to stay at Rythmia, I needed to get back to the real world. This is when much more work takes place. Integration back home the first time was very tough on me. I was coming off such a high vibration of Love and Light energy that when I was on my own again, everyone seemed negative and mean. People seemed a bit duller, but nature seemed so much brighter. Sounds were annoyingly louder, whereas healthy plant-based foods never tasted better. The morning TV show that I *needed* to turn on every morning at 7:00 a.m. and watch until 11:00 p.m. before Aya all of a sudden seemed full of doom and gloom. I felt like I did not belong in this space anymore and longed to get back to a Sacred space. I wanted to continue to feel that intense, energized feeling, and I used every tool and technique I had to sustain it, but alas, I couldn't.

So, four months after coming home from Rythmia, I signed up with Cathleen again to sit in on a ceremony, this time with Taita Juanito's brother, Taita Luis. Taita Luis is a powerful healer and seer with an infectious laugh and a sweet, gentle heart. His gift comes from plants, animals, and a place of deep wisdom passed down from his ancestors deep within the Earth and Amazonian culture. My intention was to heal my body, specifically my right kidney, which had several stones in it. For two nights, I had vivid visions and terrible pain in my hip area, then slept like the dead for the remainder of the night. One thing that I had not mentioned before was that another embarrassing (to some) side effect was that sometimes when deep into the medicine, people could release their bowels without knowing it. For some reason, while at Rythmia, I never felt a need to wear a diaper; however, with Taita Luis, I did. It goes without saying what happened during the last ceremony; I had come full circle and went back to infancy, completely letting "sh*t" go literally and figuratively, feeling complete.

It was during this trip that I was able to find my true tribe or Soul Sisters, as I call them. Having them accept me and see me for everything I am, with no judgment, no drama, no fear of Being truly, authentically seen. Friends who I just know have been my friends for lifetimes and will support me through thick or thin. They help me remain conscious, beaming with Light, Love and reminding me to stay in my feelings and intuition. I am so blessed to have had the opportunity to do Yagé with these ladies.

I went back to Rythmia in 2021, again with Cathleen. My intention was to heal my body, once again, focusing this time on specifically my Hashimoto's thyroid disease to help eliminate the need for my medicine. I had more pintas, Mother showed up as a snake again and entered my body, but most importantly, I was totally aware and in tune with every aspect of my body. I could intensely feel my heart beating. I had pins and needles, tics, huge pops, twitching, and what felt like a full night of tensing and an electric zap of every single one of my cells in my body. I had so many surgeries in these ceremonies, and I was in so much pain. At one point, the pain in my tooth became so bad my son showed up as my dentist to extract it. I believe all this body work was in preparation for releasing and healing so that my body could more fully absorb and use the stem cell infusion I chose to get at the Medical Clinic on the last day.

I also had several consultations and downloads. I talked to my father, and he explained my Starseed Light warrior lineage, which is passed from father to daughter and daughter to son, and so on, came from my paternal side. I also learned the reason my son made the decision to step away from me and set boundaries around our relationship, which had nothing to do with me directly, but that it was his own masculine trauma to heal. After having this consulta, I finally knew then that I was part of a years long lineage of ancestral healers. And that I would be asked to use my gifts and talent as a healer to live in Love and Light, not with traditional schooling, which is where my career was, but in the authority of knowing through Soul training. The wisdom that would slowly come to me would help allow me to put it all together, and that storytelling would be a part of this process.

As an overly sensitive empath, I was used to taking on other people's energy, even though I didn't know that was what I was doing. I asked Aya what I could do about this, and the vision I was shown was of myself as a person loading up non-stop luggage from a conveyor belt into a plane. At some point, Aya said, "We can do this for infinity." I refused to ask anyone for help, and it was hard! I realized at that point that the message for me was that it is not my job to lift or carry other people's luggage. I told everyone to pick up their own damn luggage and that it was not my job. I need to just say no and set strong boundaries for myself. I also saw S. and Spirit guides saying that the relationship was affecting Soul. They explained to me that I was a high vibration and bright Light that S. and others were drawn to, like a moth to a flame, and received warmth and high vibrational energy from me. While they were attracted to my physical beauty, they did not clearly see the beautiful Spirit inside me. They were consuming my Light, dimming it (which Bobby allowed them to do) to the point of almost diminishing it. But before that could happen, they would move on to someone else to seek the light in them. Bobby felt she needed to take care of these other people, but it needed to stop. Soul is here on Earth to help Others, but not to do their inner work or processing.

I received so much awareness during my Aya ceremonies that I have a deep calling to give back to the Indigenous community in Colombia. The Magic Fund[35] (Movement for Ama-

---

35. https://magicfundamazon.com/

zonian Growth and Indigenous Cultures) is a 501(c) 3 set up under the leadership of Taita Juanito to help protect and preserve the Amazon Rainforest and her peoples. Taita Juanito is a direct link and in touch with the needs and goals of the Indigenous communities and helps directly guide the initiatives. The newest initiative is Planting MAGIC[36] concentrating on the reforestation of 50 acres of land in the Amazon. For each sale of this book, I will be donating 25% of the profits to the Magic Fund and Planting MAGIC initiatives.

Awareness and Reclaiming of Reality

> "We are asleep. Our life is a dream. But we wake up sometimes, just enough to know that we are dreaming."
>
> —*Ludwig Wittgenstein*

It was all a dream. Once I saw the multidimensional Cosmos and had visited these other dimensions, I started to see things and experience things that couldn't be explained. Other than that, they were miracles. These dimensions are out of your body, out of your head, traveling to a place that can't really be explained, but I most liken it to a twilight phase; awakeness, yet drifting off into another reality. In this dimension, I see things so crystal clear I try not to make sense of them, just experience them with a wondered observation, and when I come back to this Earth's reality, I reflect on my journey.

I have changed since I did plant medicine. I think I have become calmer, surer of myself, less driven, more at peace. When COVID hit and the business world as we know it shut down, I also slowed down. I am not sure if it was due to loss of Spirit, enmeshment in my past relationship, minor depression, or if it was a sign from the Universe to everyone to shut off and regroup. I think all the above. For the past two

---

36. https://magicfundamazon.com/ways-to-help/

years I have struggled with motivation and focus, and it is uncomfortable for me. I feel guilty like I "should" be doing, working, and achieving. Knowing what I need versus what I want is still a bit tough. But I have learned that it's not what I want but what the Universe wants for me. There should not be so much forcing or pushing that goes into work and desired outcomes. Sitting in silence and flow, allowing things to come to me with the least amount of effort, and taking days or weeks off, if needed, often allows me to receive with gratitude what is meant to be. I know that the passionate, creative, knowing Spirit is still inside of me. It is just in the incubation stage, waiting to hatch.

I have also learned that being alone is not scary. Its roots mean ALL ONE. To bring oneself back together to stand tall and strong. Being quiet doesn't mean that creativity isn't brewing. For me, after a period of solitude, I often come out of it in a flourish, generating something great. I am finished trying to help Others live out their dreams and creations and ready to pick up where I left off with mine.

It is one thing to prove something and learn about something from an intellectual point of view; I have used this left brain for the majority of my life. It is quite another to be given the blessing of Spiritual knowing and Being. These are entirely new gifts that were given to me with plant medicine. To say that I have seen greatness is to say that I have seen myself as the Universe sees me. I have seen myself not as a human but as light and dusk in a never-ending vast alternative concept of reality. It was during this time that everything in my life changed. To say that Aya allowed me the biggest shift, most meaningful, profound experience of my life is unequivocally true.

My Chosen Family and Sisterhood

> "And then my Soul saw you and it kind of went, 'Oh there you are! I've been looking for you.'"
> —Iain Thomas

> "Our Spirits recognized each other when we met. I felt as though I had known her before, a feeling of déjà vu upon our meeting."
> —Dorothy Thompson

As I have alluded to in the previous section, I have a group of women that I call Soul Sisters: Cathleen, Lisa, Lauren, and Ellen. We don't live close to each other, with the exception of Lisa, and I have only known them for a relatively short time in this lifetime. I've done plant medicine with them. I've done animal medicine with them. I've laughed with them and cried with them. They get me. I feel like when I am with them; I can be myself and also bear and shed *self* until Soul appears. When I am with them, it is like the absolute first time that I get the opportunity time and time again to share my deepest, darkest secrets with no fear (well, a little fear), knowing that there will be no judgment, no shame, no blame, no resentment, no harsh questioning. I am held in Light and Loving compassion while I work through the scars on my heart. I love and trust these women, as Soul and Spirit depend on it.

I have told these women dark secrets. Secrets cause shame and guilt. Secrets generate anxiety and cause fear. Secrets disconnect us from each other and affect our most intimate relationships. Secrets are harmful to the body and our psyche. Secrets cause us to be defensive and untruthful. There is drama and trauma in the secrets we keep. I believe secrets account for 99.9% of our suffering here on Earth. While this is not statistically validated, just think about it. We all have secrets. In order to undo the pain in our cells and in our hearts and gain back Soul, we must learn to bring these hidden stories to the surface. Whether it is financial, sexual abuse, bulimia, drugs or alcohol, betrayal, unwanted pregnancy, or other desperate acts, we must feel safe to tell someone. We can't bury them forever, and if we try, we are reminded of them at the most inopportune time, and the pain starts its cycle all over again. Secrets are like cuts on Soul. If we don't deal with them, they will continue to ooze and weep and fester for years to come. If we bring them back out to the surface, cleanse them, and give them Light, it is only then that they start to heal, eventually becoming a scar. We must speak our secret stories out loud and wear these scars like a badge of truth. When the truth comes out, Soul is healed and resurrected. That is what I have done with my Sisterhood. I love them so very much and thank them every chance I get for their support in my process.

Plant Medicine: Psilocybin and Santa Maria

> "I could tell you my adventures - beginning from this morning, said Alice a little timidly: but it's no use going back to yesterday because I was a different person then."[37]

> "Nature loves courage. You make the commitment, and nature will respond to that commitment by removing impossible obstacles. Dream the impossible dream, and the world will not grind you under, it will lift you up. This is the trick. This is what all these teachers and philosophers who really counted, who really touched the alchemical gold, this is what they understood. This is the shamanic dance in the waterfall. This is how magic is done. By hurling yourself into the abyss and discovering it's a feather bed."
>
> —*Terence McKenna*

When on this quest of relinking parts of Soul, I had my first experience with psilocybin, or magic mushrooms on July 30th, 2021. It should be noted that psilocybin is a Schedule I

---

37. Carroll, L. (2021) *Alice's adventures in Wonderland*. Chapter X. The Lobster Quadrille. (p. 45). Digireads.com Publishing, e-Book. www.digireads.com

substance in the United States, making it illegal to possess.[38] However, it should also be mentioned that much scientific research has been done around these naturally occurring plant psychedelics. Johns Hopkins Medical researchers discovered that psilocybin could help relieve depression symptoms in patients for up to a month.[39] Furthermore, in an article from the US Government National Institutes of Health Medical Library, it was found that in trials of psilocybin, significant reductions of both anxiety and depression in patients were seen.[40]

The ceremony I participated in was a small one, in a beautiful backyard on air mattresses with blankets. I had two of my four Soul Sisters with me, Cathleen and Lisa. The facilitator explained what the process would look like. He would carefully measure the correct weight of the *Psilocybe cubensis* (in this case, A.P.E or albino penis envy, one of the strongest, most rare types of these mushrooms) to match our needs. I would drink it mixed with pineapple juice to help increase the digestion of it and shorten the time for the drink to take effect.

I drank my serving, and within a short time, I started to feel the changes happening. I looked back to my journal, and I did not write anything after this ceremony, but I do remember not liking it and resisting letting go with this medicine. I was in an altered state and became very paranoid that my friends were talking about me. I remember that my sense of time was severely altered; what was probably minutes seemed like eons to me, and I was worried about missing a ferry! I

---

38. United States Department of Justice Drug Enforcement Administration Controlled Substances www.deadiversion.usdoj.gov/schedules/orangebook/c_cs_alpha.pdf Retrieved June 23rd, 2022, from: https://www.deadiversion.usdoj.gov/schedules/
39. Gukasyan, et al. (2022). Efficacy and safety of psilocybin-assisted treatment for major depressive disorder: Prospective 12-month follow-up. *Journal of Psychopharmacology, 36*(2): 151–158. https://journals.sagepub.com/doi/10.1177/02698811211073759
40. Ziff, et al. (2022). Analysis of psilocybin-assisted therapy in medicine: A narrative review. *Cureus, 14*(2): e21944. https://www.ncbi.nlm.nih.gov/pmc/articles/PMC8901083/

thought I was a caterpillar, one similar to the one in Alice and Wonderland, but I was red with white polka dots, had a top hat, and a circular monocle, and as I looked up, I was in awe of the stars and the Milky Way. The next morning, I found out that the facilitator gave me the biggest dosage out of any participants, and I vowed I would never do it again.

Fast forward to the Summer Solstice on June 21st, 2022. To overcome my fear, I sat once again with my Sister Cathleen, while my other Sister Lisa, held space for me. The strain this time was Golden Teacher, and I took half the dosage as before. This time I had a mellowed-out experience seeing Sacred geometry and just feeling gratitude in Love. I am happy I had a better experience this time around; however, I can safely say that psilocybin is not my medicine of choice.

Cannabis, or Santa Maria as it is referred to in the plant medicine community, can also be used for pain management, visions, anxiety, sleep, and revealing One to Oneself.[41] I have sat in ceremony with both a microdose of psilocybin and a microdose of Santa Maria and had a profound experience. Now that cannabis is legal in Massachusetts, I have purchased gummies and mists from Rebelle[42], a dispensary in the Berkshires, to complement my supply of ritual plant medicines, but I do not partake recreationally. This is also not a medicine of choice for me, but I do believe in the healing properties of it.

---

41. Why is cannabis called "Santa Maria" In medicine circles? Retrieved on February 28th, 2023, from: https://steemit.com/cannabis/@cabelindsay/why-is-cannabis-called-santa-maria-in-my-circle
42. https://letsrebelle.com/ Please note you must be 21 years or older to enter the site.

Animal Medicine: Kambô and Bufo

> "Humans are amphibians- half Spirit and half animal. As Spirits they belong to the eternal world, but as animals they inhabit time."
>
> —C.S. Lewis

So where do I begin? This is a post from Facebook, of what I posted right after I went through this experience; it sums it up well.

For the past four days, my Soul Sisters 💗 and I have been on a HUGE life-altering personal transformation healing journey at our Retreat Center in Costa Rica. We have been WATER with a four-day-only water fast 💧, we have been AIR through our breath work 💨, we have had our bodies FROZEN 🥶 through long intense ice baths, we have altered our THOUGHTS 💭 about what is TRUE 😇, we have been marked and branded together forever (. . .) and burnt with Sacred FIRE 🔥, we have been poisoned 🐸 and HEALED 🤮 through ancestral Amazonian animal medicine, we have felt PAIN 😫 and had our SIGHT restored 👁 through knowing, we have remembered who we are 🕉 and SAW where we came from ♾🌀✴ through TRUST 🌠 and eventual DEATH💀. Only then, when our ego and physical bodies were broken down and exhausted, we were given the gift of REBIRTH 🐣 💗 and returned here on EARTH 🌍 to experience all-encompassing LOVE 💗 and LIGHT ✴. This truly has been an unforgettable rite of passage that words cannot explain. I am so grateful to my tribe of Sisters on this journey with me and to Karina Love and Niko from Plugin Mind for holding us in such Sacred space. I love you all so much ⚘ Thank you, thank you, thank you.

Sounds a bit bizarre, doesn't it? Let me break it down in a bit more detail. Kambô[43] is the name for the *Phyllomedusa*

---

43. Retrieved October 23rd, 2022, from: https://en.wikipedia.org/wiki/Kambo_(drug)

bicolor, or Amazonian tree frog. Before the Kambô ceremony, the poisonous defense secretion on the skin of the frog (it is not harmed or killed while obtaining this) is gently scraped off and put on a wooden pallet by a trained practitioner. While it is legal to possess in the U.S., it is not mandated, evaluated, or regulated by the Food and Drug Administration (FDA), and most studies highlight the harmful effects that can occur if it is not administered properly.[44] I want to make the distinction between calling something a poison versus a venom. According to current research, venom comes from an animal that is inflicted upon a victim in self-defense, whereas poison is something that the victim inflicts upon themselves.[45]

In preparation for the ritual, I practiced breath work daily, immersed myself in an ice bath (up to 10 minutes one time, did a four-day coconut water-only fast, had sananga administered in my eyes, and was asked to reflect on my life. I will explain more about sananga in the tincture section. Regarding ice baths, I tend to handle these extremely well, being able to still my mind completely and shut down my body by slowing down my heart rate, so much so that I can stay in for over 10 minutes and actually fall asleep! Please note that ice baths are not recommended without supervision, as hypothermia can occur if the participant is not carefully monitored.

Immediately before the ceremony, I was asked to drink a few liters of water quickly and to choose a place on my body where the poison would permeate my skin. In an effort to detox the body and the mind, up to five points are burned into the participants' skin with a small stick of bamboo and the secretions applied to it. I choose three (:) vertical points

---

44. Hesselink, J. (2018). Kambo and its multitude of biological effects: Adverse events or pharmacological effects? *International Archives of Clinical Pharmacology, 4*(1): 1–6. https://clinmedjournals.org/articles/iacp/international-archives-of-clinical-pharmacology-iacp-4-017.php?jid=iacp
45. Jared et al. (2021). Differences between poison and venom: An attempt at an integrative biological approach. *Atca Zoologica, 102*(4): 337–350. https://onlinelibrary.wiley.com/doi/full/10.1111/azo.12375

on my right lower inner ankle representing the masculine release side of the body. Once the poison was administered to the open wounds, within seconds I experienced a flushing of my body, a nauseous feeling, increased heart rate, and harsh vomiting. Depending on what was going on inside of your body, the facilitator of the medicine could tell by what was showing up in your bucket. A deep yellow bile color meant deep toxins cellular cleansing. A whitish foam tends to denote candida or yeast in your body. Throughout the ceremony, the poison was moistened with a spray bottle to reactivate the venom. The practitioner walked around monitoring me and telling me when to drink more water, and fairly quickly, the poison was flushed from my body. The longer I chose to keep the medicine on, the more healing dermaseptins (peptides with antibiotic properties) I would receive. When it was time, the facilitator wiped off the poison from my skin. I took part in this cycle for another three days, having the 2nd day, three points placed in an inverted triangle ▽ on my lower back, representing the alchemical water symbol of my birth sun sign, Cancer. On the 3rd day, I had my Soul Sisters mark the horizontal (. . .) left feminine receiving side of my body, on my lower ribs. Cathleen marked the first dot to always use my intuition because I met her first. Ellen and Lauren marked the second dot because they remind me of Love which centers everything, and Lisa marked the third dot to show me wisdom and healing. Not surprisingly, in Morse code, the literal encryption of (. . .), or dot dot dot, is the letter "S"[46] in my mind standing for Soul, Sister, Spirit, Sovereign, etc. At the end of the process, on the second and third days, I received the Bufo medicine.

Incilius alvarius,[47] commonly known as *Bufo alvarius* or the Colorado River toad, also secretes a defense poison

---

46. Morse code chart/table. (n.d.). Retrieved on February 6th, 2023, from: https://www.electronics-notes.com/articles/ham_radio/morse_code/characters-table-chart.php

47. Retrieved on October 23rd, 2022, from: https://en.wikipedia.org/wiki/Colorado_River_toad

from their parotoid glands. These secretions contain large amounts of both 5-MeO-DMT and bufotenin, which are considered hallucinogenic tryptamines.[48] It should be noted that 5-MeO-DMT is a Schedule I substance in the United States, making it illegal to possess.[49] It is purported that these secretions could kill an adult dog if the toad is attacked. Contrary to urban legend, and despite being portrayed in various media outlets, including Western television, over the past 20 years,[50] "licking" the toad can have grave consequences for humans. I also want to mention that the state of California has now classified this species of toads as endangered due to the practice of people taking and mishandling them during extractions, many times harming or killing the animals in the process.[51] This ecological outcome only amplifies my decision to sit in ceremony with a trained practitioner in the collection of the secretions.

Scientists and researchers are just now starting to study the effects of 5-Me0-DMT in controlled participant studies.[52] Preliminary findings across multiple studies found that patients consistently saw improved mood, reduction of anxiety, depression, PTSD, substance abuse, and obses-

---

48. Weil, A. and Davis, W. (1994). Bufo alvarius: A potent hallucinogen of animal origin. *Journal of Ethnopharmacology, 41*(1–2): 1–8. https://www.sciencedirect.com/science/article/abs/pii/0378874194900515
49. Retrieved October 24th, 2022, from: https://www.federalregister.gov/documents/2010/12/20/2010-31854/schedules-of-controlled-substances-placement-of-5-methoxy-nn-dimethyltryptamine-into-schedule-i-of
50. Once on this site, if you scroll down and open the folders, it lists every medium which toad licking has been mentioned. Retrieved on October 31st, 2022, from: https://tvtropes.org/pmwiki/pmwiki.php/Main/ToadLicking
51. Retrieved October 27th, 2022, from: https://en.wikipedia.org/wiki/Colorado_River_toad
52. Davis A.K., So S., Lancelotta R., Barsuglia J., Griffiths R.R. 5-methoxy-N,N-dimethyltryptamine (5-MeO-DMT) used in a naturalistic group setting is associated with unintended improvements in depression and anxiety. Am J Drug Alcohol Abuse. 2019;45(2):161–169. https://pubmed.ncbi.nlm.nih.gov/30822141/#

sive-compulsive disorder symptoms.[53] In one controlled study of 22 volunteers (2021), researchers found that after inhalation, *"cognitive and psychomotor functions quickly return to baseline after administration. These findings further attest to the safety profile of pharmaceutical grade 5-MeO-DMT if adequately administered in a controlled setting . . ."*[54]

Days before the ceremony, a trained Spiritual practitioner "milked" the toads' glands to release the poison collected from the animal in a comparable way to Kambô. It was then squeezed onto a piece of glass and spread around. When the secretions dried, they were scraped off with a razor into flakes and put into a small bowl with a pipe. Sitting lotus style with Soul Sisters surrounding me, I set my intention for what I wanted to realize (to remember where I came from) during this ritual. When the flakes are vaporized, a single inhalation is taken, and an immediate fast-acting (15-seconds) effect is felt. 5-MeO-DMT is 4–10 times more powerful than DMT when inhaled,[55] thus earning it the title of the "God molecule."[56]

I slowly lowered myself backward to start my peaceful journey. My ego was trying to fight the release to go into a different dimension, and Higher Spirit was telling me to let

---

53. Reckweg et al. (2022). The clinical pharmacology and potential therapeutic applications of 5-methoxy-N,N-dimethyltryptamine (5-MeO-DMT). *Journal of Neurochemistry, 162*(1); 128.146. https://onlinelibrary.wiley.com/doi/10.1111/jnc.15587
54. Reckweg et al. (2021) A Phase 1, Dose-Ranging Study to Assess Safety and Psychoactive Effects of a Vaporized 5-Methoxy-N, N-Dimethyltryptamine Formulation (GH001) in Healthy Volunteers. *Frontiers in Pharmacology, 12*: 1–12. https://www.frontiersin.org/articles/10.3389/fphar.2021.760671/full
55. Shen H, Jiang X, Winter J, and Yu A. (2010) Psychedelic 5-methoxy-N,N-dimethyltryptamine: metabolism, pharmacokinetics, drug interactions, and pharmacological actions. *Current Drug Metabolism, 11*(8): 659–666. https://www.ncbi.nlm.nih.gov/pmc/articles/PMC3028383/
56. Hasty, M. (2022). Breaking down the God molecule: Exciting developments in 5-MeO-DMT. Retrieved on November 1st, 2023, from: https://psychedelic.support/resources/breaking-down-the-god-molecule-exciting-developments-in-5-meo-dmt/

go, so I do remember my head moving from side to side as if the ego and the Soul were on either side of me, but eventually, Soul won, and I was floating, formless in a beautiful white Light. Space with nothing in it. I was One with the space, and there was no separation. I was finally pure Soul. I could *feel* the beautiful energy within me, and I started giggling, apparently out loud, because soon I heard Cathleen start giggling along with my other Sisters. Bufo is short-acting, only around 20-30 minutes or so, and all I remember thinking, as I was slowly coming back into my body, is how I wanted to go back, that it was so f*$ing beautiful! After a while, I heard one of the Sisters ask me if I was ready for a hug, and I said, "Yes, get in here!" What an incredibly powerful experience to just have had. Words do not give it justice. I experienced such an intense Love for everyone and everything much more quickly and more powerful than I had with Aya.

That evening, before bed, I knew I was still in the medicine and that I needed to release some things. The first to go was ego. Then fear, I asked vanity, jealousy, and envy all to pack up and leave my mind and body. Then I was on a dream journey, and I experienced a death. At first, I was afraid, but then I realized that in order for everything that I wanted to be released, those things had to die. Also, a lot came through about my relationships with men and how I try to be an Angel to heal them but that doesn't mean I need to have an intimate relationship with them, and that I must take care of my own healing first. Part of my healing that came from seeing the faces of my female ancestors was that they invited me to find more men that I could connect with on a deeper, meaningful Soul level.

On the last day sitting with Bufo, I was told I was going to again be the last person to receive. Ellen went first and I sat downwind from the smoke, and I must have inhaled some of her exhaled medicine. I could hardly keep my head up, and each time the other Sisters went, I took on some of their medicine. When it was finally my time, Niko said, "Wow, you are already in the medicine." He kept asking me to breathe in, and I would breathe out. He would ask me to breathe out, and I would breathe in. I finally got it right, and I was, this time, in space with beautiful mandalas. I also heard the loveliest, repeating, sighing, feminine sound of "ahhhh," coming from Angels or Soul. When I came back, I asked everyone if it was me making that noise, and they all told me no. I knew then, without a doubt, it was indeed the breath sound of the Universe. I still have awe-inspiring remembrance of illumination and pure Love remembering this. I am in gratitude. Here is where I am at a loss for any more words to describe the experience.

Both Karina and Niko from Plugin Mind,[57] took such great care and love with me and my Soul Sisters. They are both Angels serving here on Earth and will truly always be a part of Soul family. I love them both so much.

---

57. https://pluginmind.com/

PART IV:
Healing Toolkit

The Summer: Kintsugi Repairing

> "It has taken me 57 times circling the sun to realize that I am my own best teacher, lover, guru, friend, healer, and guide."
>
> —Me

Up until this point in my life now, I have allowed others to control me and how I chose to give my power away throughout my life, both in personal relationships and work relationships, and how it has unauthenticated Soul. It was only because of my deep-seated fear of being less than, being hurt, people judging me, or perceiving me as weak, that I developed habits of allowing others to use, guilt trip, or manipulate me. These limiting belief patterns and thoughts have been almost entirely eradicated now. I have learned that I need to give up the illusion of me being in control all of the time and practice being comfortable with the Universe guiding and nudging me.

In this human body, it is often a struggle to keep Spirit vibration high. I have to work at it each and every single day, just like when I was climbing back up the mountain. It takes work, and it is hard, but in the end, it is so very worth it. I have developed a toolkit of things that work for me, the things that feed my human mind and body, and Soul. While at times it may seem like I was on a magical quest to find that *one* that would work or help me, I have discovered that there are many things that I can use to bring me back to Oneness and ultimately, peace and Love.

In the previous pages, I have taken you to my rock bottom, the Fall and Winter, breaking cycles, reaching up, and seeing the hope in the Spring. Kintsugi is the Japanese art of putting the pieces of a broken object back together again with a beautiful lacquer using gold, silver, or platinum, many times making the original object more beautiful than it was before, rather than trying to hide the fractures.[1] I am using this form of golden and silver repair with Soul, continuing to relish and feel the Light and Love of this Summer season.

Quieting the Mind: Hapé, Mambe, and Tinctures

> "Quiet the mind and the soul will speak."
> —Ma Jaya Sati Bhagavati

> "Every molecule, every organism has its own prayer to the Earth . . . and the Earth listens."
> —Taita Juanito

Hapé, or rapé as it is called by ancestral people in South America, is considered a Sacred healing medicine that has been used by Indigenous tribes of the Amazon for thousands of years. It is a fine, snuff-like powder, prepared and made with prayers and intentions from a Shaman, using medicinal herbs, and many times with a tobacco base. Before receiving hapé, an intention is made. Hapé is either administered by another up the nose with a *tepi*, inserting one end of the pipe into the nostril of the person receiving, and the administrator blowing up the left side first (releasing what no longer serves) and then the right nostril (receiving what is in the best and highest good). There are double nostril pipes as well. Self-administration is possible with a *kuripe*, a V-shaped pipe. It is

---

1. Retrieved on February 28th, 2023, from: https://en.wikipedia.org/wiki/Kintsugi

extremely important that the breath is held and individuals don't swallow or breathe in the fine powder. Healing properties include opening the 3rd eye and decalcifying the pineal gland, which naturally hardens with age, purifying the digestive system by moving the bowels, cleansing the upper respiratory tract and sinuses, helping ground oneself or giving energy depending on the blend, and providing clarity and focus. It is legal to possess in the U.S.

I had read about hapé before my trip to Rythmia and realized that because of COVID, hapé would not be readily available by Shamans due to the close contact with mucous membranes and blowing of breath from another. I called Rythmia, and they explained that it is legal to possess in the U.S. and I could purchase hapé at the gift shop for self-administration, but the *kuripe* pipes were sold out, but if I really wanted to try it, I should try to bring and make my own out of a straw. I wasn't going to let this opportunity pass me by, so I packed several large green straws from Starbucks in my suitcase.

Hapé is not for the faint of heart. My first experience with it was the first night before the ceremony. Several participants and Shamans were partaking in this practice, and since Cathleen and I had purchased some hapé from the store, I dug out the straw, and we administered it *reverently* to each other. It burned my nasal cavity and made me lightheaded. It caused me to stuff right up and produce a lot of mucous. Because the fine powder goes to the back of the throat, I am constantly spitting and hacking up phlegm. Depending on the amount administered, it makes me feel a bit spacey and out of it. One time in Rhode Island, on some rocks by the ocean, I tried to stand up to move from the rock I was sitting on and tumbled down several feet!

After a Yagé ceremony, the Shamans administer hapé to anyone that wants it and let me tell you; it normally knocks my socks off. The Taitas either administer much more than I normally give myself, or it is in the technique of their blowing.

I have seen so many people almost pass out, throw up, moan, and cough, with a few even taking hours to recover.

The ones I use today are from the Nukini tribe, called Divine Mother Rose, and from the Yawanawa Tribe, called Children from the Rainforest, from Four Visions Market,[2] but I have used others that are just as effective as well. Most of the time, I purge through burping, hacking up phlegm, elimination of bowels, then I get the chills, and sense my body with wings, centering into my heart space, hearing the wind, or feeling the rain and cleansing of my body by water. I sit crossed-legged with my left palm up to release and transmute and my right palm down to receive. I go back to the place of remembering when I was in medicine, and many times, I can see Valdon's purple dragon eye through my third eye, feel helper Spirits lift me up, or see Sacred geometry. More on who Valdon is on the next few pages. After a while, I blow my nose, take a sip of water, and calmly go about my day, grounded back into Spirit.

The Sacred feminine medicine mambe is made and used by Colombian Indigenous Amazonian tribes, including Taitas and other medicine people. The word mambe means "the tongue of God: or "the word of life"[3] and is used for clear communication, giving power to words and thereby, wisdom to the one who is speaking. In ceremonies, mambe is taken with ambil. Ambil is a black indigenous paste made from strong tobacco, which can be consumed or used as a paste for healing wounds. It is legal to possess in the U.S. but not mandated, evaluated, or approved by the FDA. It stimulates the salivary glands to produce mucus before taking the mambe. Mambe or ypadu, as it is known as, is made by an unrefined process from coca leaves, mixed with the ash of yarumo leaves, and pulverized into a fine green powder. It should be noted that coca leaf is a Schedule II substance in the

---

2. https://fourvisionsmarket.com/product/divine-mother-rose-hape/
3. Mambe medicine. (n.d.). Retrieved on January 14th, 2023, from: https://almahealingcenter.com/plant-medicine/mambe-coca/

United States, making it illegal to possess. A small amount of masculine ambil is taken first, then a scoop of mambe is put in the mouth to form a paste by chewing it until it forms a ball in my cheek, so its healing properties, energy, and nutritional value are absorbed through the mucous membranes. I use mambe and ambil when authenticity and truth are needed when thinking or speaking. I swallow the mambe liquid only when absolutely necessary, and a small amount in my cheek can last hours sometimes. I use this medicine before a big Zoom call or business consultation to bring me clarity.

The Colombian Taitas, in an effort to help support their Tribes, produce and sell intricate beaded jewelry, feathered fans for clearing, hapé, natural pastes for wounds, plant bath teas, and liquid botanical tinctures to further enhance individual healing when back home. I purchased two of these tinctures to microdose when I need it, which are legal to possess in the U.S., but not mandated, evaluated, or approved by the FDA to help guide my dreams and allow me to be more heart-centered. The two that I purchased from Four Visions marketplace and that were made in the Yagé tradition with fire, water, prayer, and chants by Taita Juanito, who comes from a long lineage of ethnobotanists, were Ambi (meaning medicine healing) Sacha (meaning tree of life, for overall healing), a Yagé tincture made just from the vine of the Ayahuasca plant, and Ambi Puncha. I use Ambi Sacha to empower me and allow me to connect deeply with Spirit. I also use it to prolong healing after ceremony, grounding and reconnecting to the Cosmos with dream journeying. I use Ambi Puncha (meaning calmness or clarity) to open my heart during Spiritual transformations and strong healing.

Indigenous plant baths are something else I have used after Ayahuasca when I return home. For the first seven days, I seep pre-prepared natural ingredients like basil, tulsi, rosemary, thyme, lavender, cinnamon, and lemongrass in hot water and poured it over my body, not rubbing it off, waiting for it to dry. This is called a sweet bath to bring sweetness and strengthen Spirit. Then for another seven days, I seep different pre-prepared natural ingredients like tobacco, rue, and white sage. This is called a bitter bath to extract bitterness and help release pain and trauma. Then repeat the sweet bath for the last seven days. All baths are prepared lovingly in prayer and sustainably sourced.

When I have anxiety, in the past I have also used a few drops of Mary's Nutritionals, The Remedy, which is an elite activated hemp CBD oil extract that was recommended to me by Rob Gronkowski's former massage therapist. At the time of this writing, he does not have any affiliation with this company. It is legal to possess in the U.S. but not mandated, evaluated, or approved by the FDA. A few drops of this before bed or anytime I am feeling overwhelmed helps provide balance and reduces stress.

Sananga comes from the roots and bark of the *Tabernaemontana undulata* scrub, and it is applied as an eye drop. It is legal to possess in the U.S. but not mandated, evaluated, or approved by the FDA. I haven't purchased Sananga, but it comes in gentle, medium, and strong strengths. I have used these Sacred medicinal drops before psilocybin ceremonies, as well as after Kambô. Indigenous Amazonian tribes suggest using it for seeing life with clear eyes, physical, Spiritual, and energetic healing, and a heightened connection with Source. It stings your eyes, but within a few minutes, once you can open them, everything seems brighter and crisper. The ancestral tribes used it to sharpen their eyes before going out into the jungle to hunt.

Crystals and Chakra Balancing

> "In a crystal, we have the clear evidence of the existence of a formative life principle, and though we cannot understand the life of a crystal, it is nonetheless a living being."
>
> —*Nikola Tesla*

> "When you are realized, you can start feeling your own chakras and the chakras of other people. This is enlightenment."
>
> —*Nirmala Srivastava*

These talismans help me remember that the Spirit energy that can't be seen, especially within me. I have seven crystals that I link to the seven chakras. I clear my chakras by placing the crystals midline on my body, chanting the corresponding Sanskrit Bija mantra: red jasper (root- LAM), orange carnelian (sacral-VAM), yellow citrine (solar plexus-RAM), green aventurine or rose quartz (heart-YAM), lapis lazuli (throat-HAM), amethyst (third eye-AUM), and clear quartz (crown-OM). I start from the bottom and imagine the color rotating clockwise. I chant the Bija mantra until I can *feel* the energy swirling in that area before moving on to the next chakra.

I love all of my three birthstones, of which I wear or carry: pearl (wisdom), Russian genuine alexandrite, an extremely rare stone more expensive than a diamond, changes color naturally depending on what light you are in, and my favorite, moonstone known for its calming properties. Black onyx helps ground me and protects against bad energies. Incidentally, I also tend to wear mostly black clothing. In a research study conducted in the U.S., black umbrellas tended to block 90% of ultraviolet (UV) harmful energy rays from the sun.[4]

---

4. McMichael, J., Veledar, E. and Suephy, C. (2013). UV radiation protection by handheld umbrellas. *JAMA Dermatol.* 2013;149(6):757–758. Retrieved May 7th, 2022, from: https://jamanetwork.com/journals/jamadermatology/fullarticle/1670412

Therefore, if black can protect against incoming energy, it will also keep my internal energy and vibrations from being drained by other external sources.

I also use powerful labradorite mineral crystals, which is the stone of transformation and healing, imparting strength and perseverance. Shungite is an antioxidant with exceptional anti-inflammatory capabilities, especially electromagnetic frequencies, worn as a bracelet. Some other ones in my collection are fluorite (for dreaming), black tourmaline (protection), rose quartz (love), malachite (protection, transformation), amethyst (calming), and opalite (not naturally occurring, but helps with communication and clarity), pyrite or fool's gold (manifestation), blue sodalite (truth and inner peace), red jasper (grounding, but increases productivity), turquoise (tranquility) and prasiolite (creativity). My selenite wand I use to cleanse, purify all the other stones of unwanted energy, and recharge them. My dowsing pendulum,[5] which helps me with yes or no questions, is made from red jasper (removes obstacles). My indigo gabbro or mystic merlinite angel is technically not a crystal. It is an igneous rock, but it has strong metaphysical properties that help connect with Higher Consciousness. On my desk, I have beautiful clear and taupe chalcedony geode bookends that bring me confidence and encourage Sisterhood.[6] It is also thought to be a lucky stone for Cancer signs, aligning mind, body, and Spirit.[7]

I use a Himalayan salt lamp on my desk and indulge myself with hourly salt cave sessions.[8] Himalayan salt is said to improve mood and air quality, helping with respiratory

---

5. https://www.collegeofpsychicstudies.co.uk/enlighten/how-to-use-a-dowsing-pendulum/
6. Healing properties of the chalcedony: the grace stone. Retrieved on February 5th, 2023, from: https://soulku.com/blogs/stones-in-service/chalcedony
7. Gem notes: Gemstone information. Chalcedony meaning and properties. Retrieved on February 5th, 2023, from: https://www.firemountaingems.com/resources/encyclobeadia/gem-notes/l32y
8. https://scituatesaltcave.com/

cleansing and breathing, stress reduction, and it gives off negative ions to help offset allergens and other pollutants.

I also want to mention in this section that I use an infrared crystal sauna blanket. It has a layer of far infrared heat coils, charcoal, clay, and magnetic layer, and a base layer of amethyst and black tourmaline. In addition to helping increase serotonin levels, this blanket helps improve circulation, detoxifying the body of heavy metals and promotes deep relaxation. It has helped me with inflammation due to an Achilles injury and other general aches and pains in my body.

Yoni is a Sanskrit word meaning womb or space. A yoni egg is an egg-shaped crystal attached to a string and inserted into the vagina. These eggs, along with yoni steaming, have become more mainstream because of Gwyneth Paltrow and her company, Goop, in the past touting the advantages. Goop currently has stopped selling these items. Purported benefits include relieving menstrual cramp symptoms, strengthening pelvic floor walls, natural and Spiritual cleansing of the space, and helping to increase sacral chakra energy and libido. My yoni egg is made from rose quartz, and I have used it occasionally to help center me and increase the effectiveness of Kegel exercises. It should be noted that this practice is not recommended by OB/GYNs[9] and there is no medical research to back up the claims. Please always be aware of the risks associated with yoni eggs or steaming, which can include increased infections, burns, irritation, and possible toxic shock syndrome if left in too long.

---

9. OB/GYN is an abbreviation for obstetrics and gynecology: medical physicians, specialists, or surgeons. Retrieved February 11th, 2023, from: https://www.woosterhospital.org/what-is-the-difference-between-ob-gyn-and-gynecology/

Breathwork, Meditation, and Spirit Animals

"No, I would not want to live in a world without dragons, as I would not want to live in a world without magic, for that is a world without mystery, and that is a world without faith."

—*R.A. Salvatore*

"I believe in everything until it's disproved. So, I believe in fairies, myths, and dragons. It all exists, even if it's in your mind. Who's to say that dreams and nightmares aren't as real as the here and now?"

—*John Lennon*

Pranayama in Sanskrit can be broken down into the words "prana" (life energy) and "yama" (control). Breathwork and regulation of the breath have been scientifically proven as a way to relieve stress and are associated with many other benefits, such as decreasing blood pressure, helping improve sleep, and increasing mindfulness.[10] I have learned many different processes, including the box breathing method: inhale for 4 seconds, hold for 4 seconds, exhale out for 4 seconds, hold for 4 seconds, and continue repeating. In meditation and yoga, I have used the lion's breath, inhaling a long deep full breath through the nose, exhaling forcefully with a wide mouth, and sticking my tongue out while making a "ha" sound; alternate nostril breathing, holding one hand to the nose, pinching one nostril and breathing in the other, releasing the hold on the nose and closing that nostril off, and exhaling and breathing in from the other side, alternating sides; and my favorite, the female honey bee humming breath, I use my thumbs to close the cartilage of my ears, put the other four fingers over my closed eyes, inhale and then hum out as long as I can with my exhale. It always makes me happy after a few rounds.

---

10. Nunez, K. (2020). 7 Science-backed benefits of pranayama. Retrieved on February 2nd, 2023, from: https://www.healthline.com/health/pranayama-benefits

The Wim Hof Method[11] of breathwork alone, or combined with cold therapy, is the one that takes me many times into a different dimension, allowing me to see colors through my third eye (between the eyebrows) and get extremely clear on Spirit's purpose. It involves deep cyclic (30-40 breaths) breathing, followed by holding your breath as long as you can before exhaling. Then a 15-second held recovery breath before the process starts again. There is an app or videos to guide you. I really struggle with this breathwork because, to me, it is work, but it is the one without a doubt that gives me the most benefit for Soul work.

I can't talk about meditation without mentioning Deepak Chopra again. It was through his workshops and retreats that I first learned about five distinct types of mediation.[12] Transcendental meditation or T.M., which involves reciting a single mantra, such as Om (believed to be the most Sacred eternal sound of creation) or another series of Sanskrit words over and over, made famous by the Beatles. Mindfulness meditation consists of doing a full body scan of the body and mind to determine where stress resides, focusing on the breath to destress. Zen meditation, seated, with slowed focused breathing, chanting, or reciting of Sutras (threads of simple words) to help achieve enlightenment, which the Dalai Lama practices. Kundalini yoga uses movement, breathing, mantras, focus, and mudras or hand positions. While I don't do this type of yoga, I do practice Vinyasa Ashtanga yoga (series and flow of 12 asanas or poses) in the morning, also taught at the Chopra Center, called Surya Namaskar A (sun Salutations or greetings to the sun) while reciting corresponding Sanskrit mantras for each pose. Finally, I practice primordial sound meditation. This is based on the vibrational sound the Universe was making at the exact time and place a person was born, determined by Vedic calculations. This unique sound

---

11. https://www.wimhofmethod.com/breathing-exercises
12. Lechner, T. (2014). 5 Types of meditation decoded. Retrieved on January 31st, 2023, from: https://chopra.com/articles/5-types-of-meditation-decoded

then became my personal mantra, specific to me and not to be shared with anyone. I use it silently in meditation to get into the gap, where *no* thoughts preside.

I have also used sound bowl healing meditation, and during one of the sessions, I was holding two selenite sticks in my hands. I started shaking so violently that the facilitator had to stop the meditation as I was too sensitive to the energetic sound and crystal energy. Similarly, while in a crystal store in Sedona with my Soul Sisters, I got so overwhelmed that I had to leave and ground myself before reentering. Another time, after a sound bath healing, because I am an empath that feels, senses, and very often takes on surrounding energy, I was asked to put my hands over a bowl of water. The water started jumping and making concentric circles that everyone was asked to gather around to see just how much energy the human body could absorb.

I only just discovered the phrase "acousticeuticals," a term coined by Barry Goldstein,[13] author of *Secret Language of the Heart*. Barry is a renowned expert in the field of music, sound, and vibration. He is also globally recognized for creating music to assist in meditation, relaxation, inspiration, motivation, and transformation. He has co-produced a Grammy Award-winning track, worked with Shirley MacLaine, Dave Asprey, and Dr. Joe Dispenza, and has composed and produced music for television, film, major record labels, and top ten recording artists. For the last 30 years, he has developed specific sound protocols, techniques, and teachings that he brings to life to heal and open the heart both figuratively and literally, helping change heart rate variability. Having listened to his talent and music firsthand in a meditative state, I was completely transformed, feeling the music in every part of my body, becoming one with it on a cellular level. I saw a warm, green light enveloping me, green being the color of the heart chakra while emerging myself in the experience. Also, Barry also sequenced together and composed original music

---

13. www.barrygoldsteinmusic.com

around the mantra Om Shalom Home. This six-minute meditation recording can be accessed for free via the YouTube link below.[14] These are truly notes for the Soul.

I use a slightly different variation of his intended pattern for this. I say the word Om while opening my arms wide to the sky and allowing the energy to come through my crown chakra. While chanting Shalom (Hebrew for peace), I take all the energy coming from above and capture it in my hands to bring into my heart or throat chakra. If there is anything in those chakras that I need to release, I bring that out in the last step, HOME, acknowledging this planet I live on. With both of my arms spread wide, I transmute any energy that no longer serves me back to the Earth.

There are two Spirit animals that I have been fortunate to meet so far. The first one came after my ceremony in Sedona with the Sisters. Lauren and I were holding hands and meditating, and I had a vision of me standing in a meadow holding something up to the sky. When we were done, Lauren said a lion came to her, and immediately I realized that I was holding a cub to the sun, just like in the movie *The Lion King*. Months later, Cathleen, Lisa, and I were journeying, and a lion came to Lisa, and Lisa asked me what her name was and that she thought it started with a P. Immediately, the name Penelope or Penny came to both Cathleen and me. While I haven't worked intimately with Penny, as you will soon read in another section, she is a powerful presence of protection in my life, and I am so grateful that she came through to me.

My main Spirit animal, for now, came to me during breathwork. When linked to a Spirit animal, they guide and show what traits are possessed and embodied through their representation when they reveal themselves. I set my intention to meet mine, opened my heart, and let go of expectations. A beautiful black dragon with bright purple eyes became

---

14. Goldstein, B. and Kay, K. (2019). *The power of Om-Shalom-Home Chant-444hz.* [Video]. You Tube. Retrieved February 11th, 2023, from: https://www.youtube.com/watch?v=gBPikUQ2ezc

visible to me. Every time I feel his presence, it is for guidance, empowerment, to remember my wings and fly, or to breathe out the fire or energy that I am holding that doesn't serve me or Soul. It was several months later before he told me his name. Valdon is rooted in Old Norse[15], meaning "Victorious Lord."[16] According to Vedic astrology,[17] his moon sign is a Taurus, showing great patience and respect, and is associated with the Deity Brahma, the Creator. Brahma, one of the Triple Gods, is the Hindu God Creator, also known as the Grandfather and Father of dharma, creating the Universe and all Beings.[18] Dharma is an individual's duty to fulfill their life's purpose according to the cosmic laws of existence.[19]

Dragons are often seen as powerful ancient protectors and as Spirit animals. They are known for their wisdom, fierceness, good fortune, courage, and the ability to fly high to achieve greater heights.[20,21] Valdon is both an air and fire-breathing dragon, which allows me to be enthusiastic and fiery, oftentimes breathing out ritualistic fire breaths when ridding myself of energy that is not mine.

---

15. Retrieved on February 4th, 2023, from: https://www.nordicnames.de/wiki/Valdon
16. Retrieved on February 4th, 2023, from: https://www.names.org/n/valdon/about
17. Retrieved on February 4th, 2023, from: https://www.babynology.com/name/valdon-m.html
18. Das, S. (2019). Lord Brahma: The God of creation. Retrieved on February 4th, 2023, from: https://www.learnreligions.com/lord-brahma-the-god-of-creation-1770300
19. Retrieved on February 4th, 2023, from: https://www.merriam-webster.com/dictionary/dharma
20. Crystal. (2022). Dragon Spirit animal symbolism and meaning. Retrieved on February 4th, 2023, from: https://a-z-animals.com/blog/dragon-spirit-animal-symbolism-meaning/
21. King, B. (n.d.). Dragon Spirit guide. Retrieved on February 4th, 2023, from: https://whatismyspiritanimal.com/fantasy-mythical-creatures/dragon-symbolism-meaning/

Writing, Sage, and Palo Santo

> "There is no greater agony than bearing an untold story inside of you."
>
> —Maya Angelou, *I Know Why The Caged Bird Sings*

> "Writing is therapy for soul!"
>
> —Avijeet Das

A few things helped me with my trauma of the move into poverty, opening up and talking about it, sometimes writing in a journal, but ultimately what was most effective, was to write a chapter about it (excerpted throughout this book) in *Women Who Empower*.

Writing generates electricity in me and brings me joy. I love the feeling of anticipation that I get when I sit down at my computer and allow the words and sentences to just come. I don't have to push or force; the words just flow effortlessly. I love creating. Most of the time, the hours just slip by effortlessly. I see my daily morning writing time as a deep-rooted need for nourishment. It feeds Soul. But as with my chapter in *Women Who Empower* and in writing *Searching for Sea Glass*, I hope that others are fed as well. I hope that all who read my writings can recognize something in themselves and realize they are not alone in their thoughts, feelings, and experiences and that somewhere underneath it all, there is hope. It is my hope for you, reader, to make your way back to Soul. That you do the hard work, feel all the feelings that come up, and never stop learning about yourself: where you come from, what needs to heal, and that you recognize that you are a Divine Being first and foremost.

If I experience a block and flow is not happening, I will often stand up from my desk and clear my body, entire office, and studio space, using either sage[22] (feminine) or palo santo (heart) sticks. I have used both loose and bundled sage, held in a larger shell that I found during my travels. I do this practice reverently. Many Native American cultures believe that smudging with sage helps drive out negative energy, increase wisdom, and promote well-being. Palo santo is a wood that Indigenous communities in Central and South America use for smudging. The company I purchased from only uses palo santo from fallen trees. I start by opening a door for the congested energy to leave, and then light the sage or palo santo and set an intention for this practice. I start at the front door, saying:

"I now clear away any and all energy that no longer serves me. I welcome positive energy into my mind, in my body, in my heart, in Spirit, and in my home. I release what no longer serves me to make space for new beginnings for my best and highest good. And so, it is. Aho[23]."

I use a small feather fan (represents freedom), with an elk bone handle (representing courage and strength), with clay beads[24] created for ceremonial use; however, I was recently gifted a beautiful Eagle feather from my Native American cousin, and I now use this to fan the smoke towards the open door. I smudge myself first, starting at my feet and working my way up, clearing both my front and back. Then I start on my space. I pay particular attention to every corner of the room, doorways, mirrors, my bed, and laptop, working my way clockwise throughout until complete. After everything is cleared, I use blessing sprays, made from sustainable all-nat-

---

22. I am aware of the overharvesting of white sage in the American Southwest. For this reason, I only purchase from sustainably sourced stores and use palo santo whenever I can. Environmental preservation is a top priority to me. Retrieved on January 15th, 2023, from: https://fourvisionsmarket.com/product/agua-de-aguila-spray/

23. Aho is a Kiowa/Navajo term meaning either thank you, I agree, or Amen. Retrieved on January 14th, 2023, from: https://en.wiktionary.org/wiki/aho#Pronunciation_4

24. https://www.desireedemars.com/sacred-art-2/

ural herbs or a protection spray[25] (recommended by Taita Luis), all over my body. I finish by extinguishing the stick in the shell and get back to my writing.

Burning candles made from soy wax with natural wood wicks or incense is another way to help me set and clear my space. When lighting the candles, I set an intention (even when lighting them just for the day), and when striking the match and blowing it out I say, "haux, haux." Haux is a sacred word of power that is used for healing, honoring at the beginning or end of a prayer, or a way to say thank you.[26] I rotate the candles that I use, however; I have gravitated lately to ones that include crystals in their wax. The other day I burned a yellow citrine one (to cleanse my aura and improve clarity) with eucalyptus and lemongrass for uplifting and invigoration. I tend to use incense before my hapé practice and love nag champa agarbatti[27] to help purify and replace any unwanted energy with positive, loving energy. The brand I use also has one called Dragon's Blood, and I am being called to order it as I type.

---

25. AmbiNatural Protection spray, made by Finca Ambiwasi. Retrieved on January 30th, 2023, from: https://centroceremonialambiwasi.com/
26. Retrieved on April 2nd, 2023, from https://sacred-snuff.com/product/shamanic_snuff_haux_haux_new/
27. Soff, R. (2022). What is nag champa? 6 reasons why nag champa incense sticks are preferred. Retrieved on February 5th, 2023, from: https://incensesticks.com/blogs/news/what-is-nag-champa-6-reasons-why-nag-champa-incense-sticks-are-preferred

Full and New Moon Rituals and Cacao

> "I swear, the reason for full moons is so the gods can more clearly see the mischief they create."
> —*Michael J. Sullivan*

> "Don't worry if you're making waves just by being yourself. The moon does it all the time."
> —*Scott Stabile*

I have always had problems sleeping the night before and the night of the full moon. I toss and turn, only to finally get up to read or do something until sleep comes over me. Sleep deprivation effects corresponding to the lunar cycle have been scientifically proven.[28] Indigenous communities in Argentina have also been studied and found that waking periods are shorter, and more activity is noted later in the evening during a full moon, and even in areas of high urbanization, synchronization of sleep might depend on this ancestral hunter-gatherer remembrance through the use of artificial lights.[29]

During Full Moons, I am called to release what is no longer serving me, whether people, places, or things. I tend to clear my space first, then myself. Many times I write things down on little pieces of paper and burn them outside for them to be transmuted. Full moons are also an excellent time to fill a jar with water, put some smaller crystals in it, and lay out all my other crystals in the moonlight to recharge them and make moon water. The next morning, they all go back in their pouches, and the water is put back in the refrigerator for me to sip every time I need some love, calming, or whatever property that crystal is known for. Selenite, or any other

---

28. Cajochen et al. (2013). Evidence that the Lunar Cycle Influences Human Sleep. *Current Biology, 23*(15): 1485–1488. https://www.sciencedirect.com/science/article/pii/S0960982213007549
29. Casiraghi et al. (2021). Moonstruck sleep: Synchronization of human sleep with the moon cycle under field conditions. *Science Advances, 7*(5): 1–8. https://www.science.org/doi/10.1126/sciadv.abe0465

crystal that ends in *"ite,"* and other soft or porous stones should never be placed into water, as they can dissolve or leach, and the water might be harmful for human consumption.[30]

During new moons, I am called to manifest for my highest good. I burn incense and write things down, saying them out loud and putting them into a little container until these thoughts come to fruition. Every time I reread them, even during the next month's new moon, I am always surprised by how many have been fulfilled for me. Not long ago, I honored my ancestral lineage, writing down my parents, Grandparents, Great-Grandparents, etc., on both sides of the family to remember and ask them to help in the manifestation of my path here on Earth.

Ceremonial-grade cacao is well-known by the ancient Mayans for its Spiritual significance. The *Theobroma* or cacao plant is one of the most honored plants, and the name means *"the food of the Gods."*[31] This plant is used to make chocolate, so it is legal to possess in the U.S. Please check the labeling on the products purchased, only some are FDA mandated, regulated, or approved. I make and drink cacao during full and new moon ceremonies. I first set an intention and honor the plant by giving gratitude. Then I try to make an offering back to the cacao, the Earth, or water, etc. Cacao is a heart-opening medicine that helps me experience an awakening and gives me an inner appreciation for all that is.

---

30. Young, O. (2022). Water Safe Crystals: What crystals can and cannot go in water. Retrieved February 10th, 2023, from: https://consciousitems.com/blogs/practice/water-crystals-what-crystals-can-go-in-water

31. Retrieved on February 10th, 2023, from: https://en.wikipedia.org/wiki/Theobroma_cacao

Shadow Work

"Only when we are brave enough to explore the darkness will we discover the infinite power of our light."

—*Brené Brown*

I have always either run away from my problems or ran to someone. I either flee physically, plan out new fun activities with people, or seek out new relationships to help me get over the old ones. But I learned it was time to stop running away and instead run towards and turn inwardly.

Shadow work is often associated with the dark, negative aspects deep within the psyche. However, shadow work can also be the reckoning of the beautiful parts of ourselves that we have failed to nurture. My work with my shadow first involved my negative trauma traits. For me, it was putting a mirror up to myself and asking how I had contributed to the problems I was facing. If I found myself irritated with a trait in another person, I needed to ask myself why I was being triggered by that. Most likely, it had something to do with my past, or that person exhibited a trait that I also had in myself that was considered negative.

The beautiful shadow work that I am continuously working on is to give myself permission to be a glorious Divine Soul without diminishing or dimming my Light for or in front of others.

While I was in this deep shadow work process of forgiveness in meditation, a vision came through where I was surrounded by women who I had a problem with, or they had a problem with me. I recall seeing two men in this circle of women. Instead of getting anxious and tense and getting up and running away, I stood up and told everyone that I was sorry, "*mea culpa,*" and that I loved them. I then looked at the men and told them to leave so that we could bond and love each other. Usually, before such significant visions, I see Sacred geometry, or in this case, I was streaming a TV show on my phone, and as I was falling deeper into the practice, the faces of the characters became animated in bright colors. The best way I can describe it is like a Snapchat or Instagram filter. This is plant medicine starting to work before I even partake in a ceremony! The minute I decide to sign up, book, or say yes to plant or animal medicine, the awareness, hard work, and visions start coming.

I can't remember a time when looking deep inside myself; I cried so many tears. It is because, for years, I have kept them inside of me. On that morning, after my hapé practice, I could feel and hear the rain coming down, cleansing me. And then the tears started. I was not only crying for myself and my ancestral lineage, but I was crying for humanity in general. Getting rid of the hurt and the pain, expelling it out of my body with my tears, or exhaling it out like a dragon exhales fire. Tears represent a cleansing process of the Soul and help call in Spirit guides for protection and help with creation. For me, they are like ointment to my heart, helping repair it, sealing in Light once again for protection. They also help me with initiation into other dimensions.[32]

I had stuffed my secrets down out of fear of being ridiculed and ostracized. I was taught at a young age that secrets must never be revealed. Whether I heard this from my parents or my friends, I took on the weight of the world whenever I kept a secret to myself. In the case of me holding onto the secret of growing up in poverty after I started to speak it more freely and ultimately write it down to share with the world, I realized that it wasn't something to be afraid to disclose, but rather it was a heroine's journey to share with others! I know that I was powerless to fix the situation and too young at the

---

32. Scientists generally use 10 dimensions along with string theory to explain where gravity and the light from the electromagnetic spectrum meet. However, the 6th-12th+ dimensions are considered to be metaphysical realms.
Robinson, R. (2022). How many dimensions are there in the Universe? Retrieved on January 14th, 2023, from: https://now.northropgrumman.com/how-many-dimensions-are-there-in-the-universe/

time to comprehend that, and from age 12–55, I held many secrets that caused me not to live authentically. The secrets corroded Soul, and oftentimes did not allow me to act correctly, often doing or saying things that caused more secrets.

Most recently, I attended a 3-day workshop on ancestral healing. While during the ceremony, I had explored my paternal ancestry, I had not done any work on my maternal side. I knew that most of the trauma came from this lifetime, yet I also knew I had to do some work around my mom and my unborn sister. I reached out to my cousin Susie asking her if she remembered anything about the pregnancy, the birth, or the burial. Her reply was,

> *"It was very hush, hushed. All I knew was she had been pregnant. Everyone was crying, and my mom told me that my baby cousin had gone to heaven. Other than that placard at the cemetery, that's all I know. Family secrets in the Chmielecki family were very huge. I wish I had more info. All I do know is when you were born; there was a huge celebration."*

I wondered at that moment if I was carrying around some survivor's guilt in my body. Why did she have to die; so I could live? I know she was incarnated into a fetus and chose not to be born in this lifetime, but it was still sad for me. I had so many mixed feelings about it: gratitude, longing for a biological sister, guilt, and a responsibility to live my life's purpose. No wonder I always felt so special and adored by everyone. I also know that a lot of my anxiety and stress is not mine, but it came from a cellular level from my mom while she was pregnant and was passed on to my daughter as well. I set out to clear this inner child wound during a full moon ceremony of release. Cleansing my space, tapping while releasing these thoughts, connecting with my guides to bring peace and awareness surrounding this, helping to heal not only my inner child wounds that I received *in utero*,[33] but also healing future maternal generations as well.

Anger, Grief, and Forgiveness

> "To forgive is to set a prisoner free and discover that the prisoner was you."
>
> —*Lewis B. Smedes*

> "True forgiveness is when you can say, 'Thank you for that experience.'"
>
> —*Oprah Winfrey*

Anger usually comes from a loss of hope, and fear of the unknown, revealing itself as chronic pain in the body, cyclic thinking, or ruminating in the mind. Everyone experiences anger, and there is a time and a place for it, but the work I must do is to realize that whatever is coming up, is coming up to come out. Often I think I have gotten over my anger, only to have it bubble back up again, triggered by a recent experience or what happened to me with my life-altering move as a pre-teenager. Other times I am dealing with ancestral trauma, going back hundreds or thousands of generations.

My anger has always been about being silenced or not being heard. I was afraid that I would become invisible as soon as I opened my mouth. Most of the time, I allowed the anger to flow from me. I would yell at the top of my lungs, pick so many fights, throw things, exert my will and control over people, overstep boundaries, cry, and guilt trip people, becoming punitive in nature. The problem with this is that I was exhibiting lashing out the majority of the time. I did not know how to self-regulate or allow this anger to flow out of me without externally scorching everyone in my path. Then after my first experience with meditation, I decided to

---

33. Latin, meaning "in the uterus."

just stuff it down and suffer in silence, outwardly becoming calm and okay with everything, playing nice, a happy, people-pleasing person avoiding confrontation. It was because of this that I allowed others to slowly intrude on my boundaries, strip away my instinctive nature, and to make themselves a number one priority in MY life. But I couldn't ignore this rage in myself because if I continued to stuff it down and forget about it, or didn't allow it to flow out, I would blow up in a huge fit, devastating the bonds of my relationships. While I was raging at others, the anger was also taking a toll on me, both physically (inwardly) and emotionally (outwardly). When I was younger, the anger manifested itself outwardly through bulimia, drinking and drugs, and the worst anxiety and uncontrollable energy. I used to attribute this to being high Spirited and passionate, but it was so clearly a defense mechanism for physical release. I also couldn't allow my body to hold onto it, on a cellular trauma level, because of the adverse effects it had. When I got older, this resentment was held in my body with an inflamed Achilles tendon, heart palpitations, joint pain, Hashimoto's thyroid autoimmune disease, and the formation of two tiny kidney stones appeared on my right side.

While I am re-reading the above paragraph (in 2021), tears are streaming down my face, my chest is getting tight, and I find myself holding my breath. Crying and sadness are a form of therapy in and of itself. There was so much anger inside of me that I still needed to cleanse, heal, and remember to release. I know now that I was using rage as a way to empower myself. To become big and have people listen to me because, so often, I felt unheard or misunderstood.

In order to heal, I needed to acknowledge this anger and learn how to forgive. When I learned to forgive, I was able to step back into the power of Spirit. I'm talking not only about forgiving others but also about forgiving ourselves. When I did so, I learned to live my life for myself, not others. I learned to live instinctively. My life becomes effortless and easy, allowing things to manifest for my greatest good. I was better able to choose relationships that nurtured me. I was more attuned to my natural rhythms, and I was able to ebb and flow with ease.

Forgiveness takes time. I had to work on it day-by-day, expressing gratitude and acknowledging my emotions, eventually having them fade away. But it takes day by day work! I don't think of forgiveness in terms of the other person. I see forgiveness as a gift to myself so that I can move forward, break the cycle, and release these so-called negative emotions. In order for me to forgive, I needed to take a step back. I needed to remove myself from the situation, out of sight, out of mind. I needed to cry. I needed to rage. I needed to rest. I needed to play. Flashbacks about the person and the event can come rushing over me at any given time, but I have learned to stop what I am doing and acknowledge the feeling and get to the bottom of what it is that is really troubling me about this. Most of the time, I talk to my inner child. We all have an inner child within us that craves being nurtured and attended to. If I don't tend to my inner child, I start to look for what they crave in the outside world. I've realized that in the past, I've craved attention and significance in life in the hopes that I would feel worthy, whole, and complete. But as I've done the shadow work, I've realized that looking for validation and worthiness on the outside stemmed from a childhood wound of not feeling seen as a child and feeling unworthy. So during this process, I ask myself some questions. Am I upset because my ego was slighted? Am I mad because this triggered me and reminded me about something else that happened in my past? Having a dialogue with me, always talking out loud, enables me to work through the issue. Only then can I start to become detached from it? And when I am detached from something, I give it less power and meaning in my life. When there is no power and meaning behind something, it is so much easier to forgive it and let it go.

Letting go has been the most difficult for me. I have done cord cuttings and balloon releases, setting fire to paper, but by far, the most effective for me was to journey. Many people have different definitions of what journeying means to them. To me, it means sitting in silence, allowing my dragon wings to appear, flying to a person or up to another dimension, embracing either myself or them with Light and Love, containing this bright energy in compassion, and coming back home. Allowing them to release and do what is for the good of them, myself, and the highest good of the Universe.

Another visualization that works well for me is that I try to consciously refuse to feed the fire of limiting thoughts or beliefs so that they slowly lose their flame and dwindle down into embers and, finally, cold ashes, which will be blown away in the wind and forgotten about in my mind. Only then can a new, creatively energetic thought beneficial for Soul take its place.

I sometimes also have a tough time keeping the consciousness of joyous reality when I am around people who drain my energy, are negative or mean, or unawake. The visualization that I use in this case is cord cutting. I close my eyes and imagine this person standing in front of me. I smile at them. Slowly they begin blowing up, like Violet in the movie *Willy Wonka and the Chocolate Factory,* attached to me by a cord in the middle of my body. When they are far away from me, floating in space, I thank them for the time we had together, trying to focus on the lesson learned from them, sending them Love and Light, and symbolically cutting them away from my body.

One thing that I did before my Kambô and Bufo rebirth ceremony was to take a piece of paper, or several in my case, and draw a timeline, or history if you will, about everything in my life that I could remember that caused me anger. On one side, I put either overlooked healing or absolved trauma and healed. I was not going to deny or ignore my hurt any longer. I went back to all the overlooked hurts and then allowed myself to cry, to rage, to yell, and release these things and let them go. I kept doing this until everything in my life was healed to the best of my ability. It was only through acknowledging this timeline of hurts that I was able to move from anger to blame, to shame, to grief, to release through truth, and finally to healing. Healing was forgiving myself.

Throughout this last process, I was able to release the energetic blockages, pain, and inflammation in my Achilles, joints, and chakras.

With any of these letting go ceremonies, they allowed me to let go of my ego and get centered on why I was here on this Earth. What truly was my purpose and passion? The answer is always the same. To be Love and Light, serving myself and Others by utilizing the gifts I have been given for the highest good.

Boundaries

> "Boundaries define us. They define what is me and what is not me. A boundary shows me where I end and someone else begins, leading me to a sense of ownership. Knowing what I am to own and take responsibility for gives me freedom."
>
> —Henry Cloud

People have been drawn to me all of my life. I am not sure if it is my smile, my airiness, or my aura. Most of the time, I feel like people need me, not in a good way, but rather in a demanding way. I am extremely empathetic to these lost Souls and have always felt it my job to fix, help, or save them. I tend to give and give so much of my Light, many times to the dark that eventually, my flame diminishes almost to the point of burnout.

Past relationships have taught me to steal back my time, my energy, my Light, fill my cup to the brim and be very selective about who I give a drop to. If my voracious ego ruled my life for the past 43 years, I am bound and determined to have Soul lead the rest of this life. As a human, I can't get rid of the ego, as much as I may try, but I can lead with heart versus head.

No matter whatever type of boundary exists, mine have been breached in some way. Whether it is a physical boundary (my space), a mental boundary (my thoughts), a sexual boundary (my body), a time boundary (my time), a speaking boundary (my secrets), a material boundary (my things),[34] there has been a violation. I am sure I breached others' boundaries well. But once I decided it was high time to set clear, healthy boundaries for me, I would make sure others upheld and adhered to them as well. I learned about how I could go about doing this, and what I discovered was I just needed to decide what I needed and wanted and hold true to that. What did I need to do? Most of all, I needed to say "no" to people, places, and things that no longer served me. No is a complete sentence; no explanations needed. If someone couldn't accept that, it was their decision. I could choose to walk away from them, which is also a form of a boundary. They would no longer be allowed in my space.

I still am working so very hard on setting boundaries to make me feel peaceful, feel respected, heard, and secure in my decisions. I will no longer allow myself to give away my power, energy, or Light to others. I will no longer try to make anyone else happy but myself. I will no longer allow others to make me feel less than by their words or their behaviors. I will no longer accept people's opinions, judgments, and decisions about me. I will no longer receive less than I deserve. One way I do this is to visualize that I am full of Love and Light and form a Light bubble around me and have it spread out into the room, space, city, world, and Universe, transmitting Love to offset lower vibrations.

---

34. Tawwab, N. (2021). Set boundaries, find peace: A guide to reclaiming yourself. Penguin Random House. https://www.amazon.com/Set-Boundaries-Find-Peace-Reclaiming/dp/0593192095/

Failure and Rebirth TEDx Talk

"Each night, when I go to sleep, I die. And the next morning, when I wake up, I am reborn."
—*Mahatma Gandhi*

"Our greatest glory is not in never failing, but in rising every time we fail."
—*Confucius*

"Whether we remain in the ash or become the phoenix is up to us."
—*Deng Ming-Dao*

The death and loss of security, financial safety, and my childhood home was considerable trauma in my younger life. It was embedded in my physical body, and my cells remembered this. I suffered greatly for holding on to this; by hiding it, lying about it, and pretending it did not happen. What I needed to do was learn to rid my body and rewrite the memory of it, accept it, and let it go.

Only 40-plus years later, after healing considerably, I was able to write my chapter in *Women Who Empower,* but more cathartically, I was given the opportunity to speak to this on stage in a TEDx talk.[35] The following paragraphs explain more of my healing growth.

Imagine you are a senior getting ready to graduate, and you fail a big midterm in a required course. How many of you would feel afraid? A little freaked out? Embarrassed? Not a student? What would happen if you took a risk in a business venture and lost $50,000? Same feelings? Afraid? Devastated? Anxious? How about if you are a parent? COULD you allow your child to fail? Well? I want you to fail. I want each and

---
35. TEDx talk given on April 16th, 2022, at Bentley University. https://www.youtube.com/watch?v=fYDW9nKT0AU

every one of you listening (reading this) to fail. I want you to have the most epic failures in your life numerous times.

Think I'm kidding? Just ask my current managerial communication students. All 40 of them just failed their midterm. For the past six years, I have purposely designed this class to set them up to embrace failure. They hand in deliverables, write one-page papers, do presentations, and receive zeros on all of them while providing them with only negative feedback, focusing on what they have done wrong. Everything they have learned in academia is thrown out the window. For most of them, this is the first time that they have repeatedly failed at anything. This is very frightening to them and so frustrating because ALL of us are afraid of failure.

You might be asking yourself, at this point, why anyone would take my class or hire me as a consultant. But what if we lived in a world where NONE of us were afraid to fail, ever? What if people and businesses could become motivated to embrace and overcome the fear of failure? Because this is how we learn. Through teaching that failure can result in rebirth, new creation of ideas and solutions, that the more times we fail, the less scary it becomes, and the end result can be a major transformation.

Rebirth can be defined as the act of being reborn. To many, it might mean growth, transformation, and renewal. This is creation, decline, and rebirth, and it is a continuous cycle in our lives.

Here are some examples of the cycle of rebirth. In nature: A single blade of grass can grow after a devastating wildfire. In fiction: A single phoenix that lives 500 years self-destructs by setting itself on fire, only to emerge as a younger bird. In symbols: Celtic triskele- a circle with three waves having no beginning or no end; a lotus seed struggling to grow from the depths of the mud only to break the surface, blooming into a beautiful flower only to drop its seed back into the mud to start this process all over again. Or the scarab beetle, which the Egyptians associated with the sun, traveling across the sky until the sun set and the beetle died, only to be reborn *when the sun rose again in the morning. In Businesses, take Airbnb, for example. Silicon and Angel investors thought it was an awful idea. They didn't understand the concept and would not invest. The founders scrambled to make ends meet, so they worked designing cereal boxes until investment backing came through. Today it's valued at $103 BILLION. In religions like Hinduism and Buddhism, it's called samsara, represented by the karmic birth, death, and rebirth cycle. In Christianity, specifically Catholicism, it is symbolized by Jesus rising from the dead, and we celebrate Easter.*

I have two stories that I want to share with you regarding my personal fears or experience with failure. The first story wasn't my fault. I was the product of my circumstances, yet because of this, I was SOOO fearful of financial failure that I carried it with me most of my life.

When I was younger, I grew up in an upper/middle-class family with three younger brothers and two parents. Every day I enjoyed the security of the necessities in life, and I felt safe and secure. Until one day, I didn't. My Grandmother died, and as a result, we lost our house, and soon thereafter, my dad lost his job. I ended up moving to rural northern Wisconsin, living in a three ROOM, not three bedrooms, three room cabin with no running water in the 1980s.

And because of that, I would consider this my rock bottom for many years. I became a perfectionist, a worry wart, overachiever, anxious, never wanting to experience financial despair again. But it limited me, always trying to be successful. I became unhappy---from not picking the right major, almost flunking out of college, working in jobs I hated just for the money, to going through a devastating divorce, I realized I could NOT be successful 100% of the time.

Only then did I decide to stop fighting failure. And only by recognizing and riding these waves of failure are we able to see how powerful the lessons of failure are. In hindsight, any failure in our lives, many times, turns out to be the greatest opportunity for growth.

The reason it took me almost 40 years to overcome this

fear of failure is that according to a Harvard Medical School study, [36] the emotion of DREAD only takes a tenth of a second to take root in your body and can live there a lifetime.

The second story that I want to tell you about is a figurative death and being reborn. Over the past two years, I have had the opportunity to study with some Shamans from Colombia and sit in on their Ayahuasca ceremonies. The Taitas believe that drinking a ceremonial tea will allow you to let go of your physical body, experience death figuratively and live temporarily in your astral Soul. This figurative death is very common in these ceremonies, and many participants have a deep-rooted fear of dying. They experienced apprehension, chaos, panic, and FIGHTING this inevitable death in the ceremony.

For me, knowing that fear lives in our head and our body, but doesn't live in our heart or Spirit, knowing we LEARNED to be fearful somewhere, allowed me to have a more positive experience. To welcome this "death" and get into heart, I saw myself being buried, and resigning myself to this fact, becoming comfortable with the unknown, allowing it to just happen, and then being reborn: and feeling the peacefulness, the beauty, order, and the courageousness of that moment.

It is my hope that these two stories showed you that SOME solutions to failure are about learning to reframe what failure means to you, getting comfortable with fear, and having the willingness to take chances. For some of you, it could be as simple as not going back to the corporate world and starting that business you always dreamed of doing. For parents, it could mean silently watching their child fail over and over again without stepping in to help them. For students, it might mean failing that class (pausing), which, in the end, doesn't happen to any of my students. They all end up not only surviving but thriving. Whatever it is, only you can make the decision to rise from the ashes.

---

36. Menting, A. (2022). The science of emotion. The chill of fear. Dread requires only a tenth of a second to take root. *Harvard Medicine. The Magazine of Harvard Medical School.* https://hms.harvard.edu/magazine/science-emotion/chill-fear

I'm Dr. Roberta Pellant, and as a Professor, Consultant, and parent, I want everyone listening (reading) to go out and fail at one thing today. By doing that, your future will never look better. Thank you.

—*Excerpted from my TEDx Talk on April 16th, 2022, Bentley University.*

I still struggle with fear and the killing of or the death of what must die, Just like some individuals with Ayahuasca. Psychological courage is overcoming the loss of the psyche, or in this case, mind and what others think, and the acceptance of this death by coming back to Soul.[37] The big one for me is the thoughts about marriage, how society views and values it, and the long-held security blanket of being in a marriage in order to make me feel safe. This happens especially when I doubt my happiness or get tired of taking care of myself.

The Body: Supplementing, Detoxing, and Intermittent Fasting

"You can take no credit for beauty at sixteen. But if you are beautiful at sixty, it will be your Soul's own doing."

—*Dr. Marie Stopes*

"Medice, cura te ipsum."

—*Jesus, Luke 4:23*

"Physician, heal thyself."

—*Hippocrates*

I decided a while ago to take back my human body, both in a sexual way with or without a partner and also in a physical, holistic way as well. The Divine feminine Soul representing

---

37. Putnam, D. (2004). *Psychological courage*. University Press of America.

Goddess sexuality is slowly being brought back by laughter among other Divine feminine Beings, dance, moving my body and hips, awareness of pleasure, and certain foods. It is the fire that is in my sacral chakra getting hotter. I am unblocking the energy and slowly allowing it to heat up in me. When this happens, an orangish-yellowish light and energetic swirling occurs, and I am very cognizant of it. Hypersensitive to that which needs to be more open. Not for any other person other than myself. It is feminine Soul medicine that heals the other aches and pains that have been lodged within my cells throughout generations. Slowly but surely, I am becoming the Goddess I have always known I am.

I am also learning to heal my body with nutrient-rich, whole-food, plant-based foods. No gluten, no dairy, no meat (only the occasional piece of wild-caught seafood), no pre-packaged foods, minimal sugar, little to moderate alcohol, abstaining sometimes for months on end. I try to stay away from harsh chemicals in my cleaning supplies, body/hair washes, and makeup. I use fluoride-free toothpaste. I take a daytime and nighttime multivitamin[38] and receive a B12 shot once a month because of my vegan/vegetarianism. Depending on what my body is telling me, I have just learned to listen to it. If I can't sleep, I take magnesium. If I am anxious, I take ashwagandha or triphala. If I eat something inadvertently, like gluten, or can't resist that piece of cheese, or eat seafood, I take an upper digestive enzyme from Rootcology,[39] called Betaine with Pepsin. If I have lower digestive issues, I take S. Boulardii, a probiotic from the same brand. I even take a hair supplement[40] to help slow the loss of hair pigment or gray, as I don't color my hair. In the past, I did highlight my hair;

---

38. https://www.amazon.com/Healthycell-Natural-Aging-Multivitamin-Probiotics/dp/B00COQYGVC
39. Rootcology products are developed by Dr. Izabella Wentz, PharmD, FASCP, a #1 New York Times bestselling author, who struggles with Hashimoto's disease. Her book and products can be found at: https://rootcology.com/
40. https://areygrey.com/

however, since taking these supplements, I have found that I don't need to do so any longer. Finally, every night before bed, I take a telomere lengthening supplement by Healthycell.[41] Please note that vitamins, minerals, and supplements are not mandated, evaluated, or approved by the FDA.

Telomeres are sequences of DNA found at the end (caps) of chromosomes, and their purpose is to protect the genetic information; and are largely responsible for determining life expectancy, as they tend to shorten with age.[42] Shorter telomeres are associated with disease, some forms of cancer, and the overall rate of the aging process. Medical researchers have determined that human lifestyle factors, such as what we eat, can affect the shortening or lengthening of telomeres.[43] This means *we* are in control of our aging process. While I can't stop the aging clock, I do want to slow it down by being the healthiest, most vibrant me! Thus, I started to learn about detoxing.

It should be noted that detoxing or strict dieting is not recommended, and the supervision and approval of a medically licensed physician should always be sought before undertaking any kind of diet. That being said, I have done practically every type of detox known, starting with the cabbage soup diet and the master cleanse. I have done gallbladder, liver, adrenal, kidney, gut, and harsh parasite detoxes. I have gone through "die-off" symptoms such as fatigue, achy joints, headaches, swollen lymph nodes, brain fog, and nausea. I have taken herbal pills, teas, extracts, activated charcoals, and clays to bind heavy metals, even going as far as removing every last silver mercury filling in my mouth in an effort to restore my body back to manufacturer settings. Herbs,

---

41. https://www.healthycell.com/products/telomere-length
42. Shammas M. (2011). Telomeres, lifestyle, cancer, and aging. *Current Opinion in Clinical Nutrition and Metabolic Care.* 14(1):28–34. https://www.ncbi.nlm.nih.gov/pmc/articles/PMC3370421/
43. Blackburn, E. and Eppel, E. (2017). *The telomere effect: A revolutionary approach to living younger, healthier, longer.* Grand Central Publishing, New York. https://www.amazon.com/Telomere-Effect-Revolutionary-Approach-Healthier/dp/1455587974

mixtures, charcoals, and clays are not FDA mandated, evaluated, or approved, and can be harmful if ingested or used improperly. Further research allowed me to stumble on the single, most effective reset with the least amount of discomfort, intermittent and intuitive fasting.

In his book *The Longevity Diet* (2018), Dr. Walter Vongo discovered new science to help with stem cell activation and regeneration, effectively slowing the aging process and helping fight disease while optimizing weight.[44] From his decades-long, clinically tested research, he created a 5-day fast mimicking diet called Prolon.[45] As food, Prolon does not need FDA approval; however, it is recommended to seek the supervision and approval of a medically licensed physician before purchasing. The plant-based food protocol provides all of the essential vitamins and nutrients the body needs while simulating a fast, eventually leading to autophagy. Autophagy (self-eating), or cellular cleanup of old, damaged, or abnormal cells, plays an integral role in maintaining homeostasis or equilibrium in the body.[46] Additionally, it is thought that autophagy can help prevent bacterial and viral infections, autoimmune and inflammatory diseases, and even starve off certain types of cancers.[47] Autophagy is such an important mechanism in the study of health and longevity it won the Nobel Prize in Physiology or Medicine in 2016.[48]

---

44. Longo, V. (2018). *The longevity diet: Discover the new science behind stem cell activation and regeneration to slow aging, fight disease and optimize weight.* Penguin Random House. https://www.amazon.com/Longevity-Diet-wellness-watchword-nutrition/dp/1405933941
45. https://prolonfast.com/
46. Khandia et al. (2019). A Comprehensive Review of Autophagy and Its Various Roles in Infectious, Non-Infectious, and Lifestyle Diseases: Current Knowledge and Prospects for Disease Prevention, Novel Drug Design, and Therapy. *Cells.* 8(7): 674–738. https://www.ncbi.nlm.nih.gov/pmc/articles/PMC6678135/
47. Ibid.
48. Levine B. and Klionsky, D. (2017). Autophagy wins the 2016 Nobel Prize in Physiology or Medicine: Breakthroughs in baker's yeast fuel advances in biomedical research. *Proceedings of the National Academy of Sciences of the United States of America,* 114(2): 201–205. https://www.ncbi.nlm.nih.gov/pmc/articles/PMC5240711/

I have done Prolon for the past three years. It is recommended that Prolon is done every 25 days for three months consecutively, no more frequently or any longer unless under medical supervision. The meal kits vary per day but contain teas, vitamins, nut bars for breakfast, two soups, two packets of olives or one pack of kale crackers, and a chocolate crisp treat every other day. On days 2–5, I add an amino acid glycerol drink to my tea to help preserve lean muscle mass. On day one my body transitions to a fat-burning state to help with cellular repair. At the end of day two, my body is in ketosis or complete fat burning. Day three is when autophagy occurs. More ketones are produced by the liver, so fat burning increases. On days 4–5, cellular renewal is happening at a greater rate, making my cells healthy and slowing down the aging process. On day 6, I transition back to regular food, slowly and in smaller quantities. I am rarely hungry during this fast; it just takes discipline. While weight loss is not a particular goal of mine on Prolon, I am always happy when the scale shows I am down 4–7 pounds, which stays off.

When not on Prolon, I use intermittent and intuitive fasting. I stop eating at 8 p.m. in the evening, and when I wake up, I have decaf coffee with a small amount of Nutpod creamer until 12 p.m., my first meal of the day, eating and drinking within this 8-hour period of time. I repeat this 16:8 cycle almost every day, as that is what works best for my body. I read about intuitive fasting, or learning to listen to what your body really wants, from a book by Dr. Will Cole, [49] and it resonated with me. I know that if I am hungry, I always start with drinking water or herbal tea because most of the time, when my body needs food, it actually needs fluids the most.

As I write this, while I have had several lithotripsies to rid my right kidney of the stones, I am now 100% completely free of them. I have also significantly been able to taper

---

49. https://www.amazon.com/Intuitive-Fasting-Four-Week-Intermittent-Metabolism/dp/059323233X

down my thyroid medicine with the help of my endocrinologist and continue to do so every six months. I recently went in for a blood test, and I had no evidence of Hashimoto's antibodies in my system. I was able to eradicate my autoimmune Hashimoto's antibodies to 0. While Western medical physicians will not say that this disease has been eradicated, cured, or even in remission, my intuition is telling me something else. I have no doubt that through plant and animal medicine, stress-relieving practices, and lifestyle and dietary changes, these practices played a considerable role in reversing the "dis" ease in my physical body and mental mind. I have learned to be accepting of healing energy, allow it in for aches and pains, and believe in the power of "heal thyself." I am still on a small dosage of Tirosint for low thyroid function, but I am slowly weaning off it with the guidance of my Endocrinologist. Full disclosure: at the end of 2021, I had a single 50 million intravenous (IV) dose of stem cells[50] infused into my body in an attempt for an even greater reboot to my system. It was done with umbilical cord blood in a loving, calm, peaceful medical space with sound bowls and meditations surrounding me.

---

50. Nova Cell Health at Rythmia, CR which houses a fully licensed, government backed medical facility administered the transfusion. The donor of the umbilical cord stem cells signed a consent for collection, were screened for donor eligibility and the stem cells themselves were screened against infectious diseases and for viability quality by Provida Banco De Células Madre, an FDA Registered company. https://bsuprovida.net/ Note: Costa Rica has some of the best stem cell treatment centers in the world. https://stemcellstransplantinstitute.com/2017/02/22/stem-cells-treatment-costa-rica-one-best-health-care-world-2017/

Oracle Cards, Angels, and Dreams

> "We see you in the perfection that you are. We are aware of your experiences of learning compassion and love, the emotional learning of the Earthly human experience. We are here to assist you in the process, evolving into that full awareness of the master that you are... If you could see yourselves as we see you, there would be no discontent."
>
> *—THEO*

In the past, I had lost myself so much that I didn't know how to think, nor had I fully developed the use of my intuition. I am still in the process of learning how to listen to Soul, quieting the mind, and allowing what is deep in Spirit to surface. But there are times when I call or text the Soul Sisters and ask them if anything is coming through for them for me or a particular situation. They will tap into their unique gifts, and provide me with a reading, take me through a Shamanic journey, or innately reply upon a hit that they received from their guides or the Universe.

I sometimes pull cards during hapé. I use one of three decks (Sacred Rebels, Dragon Path, and Unshakeable Inner Peace), and they help provide me with the direction I should focus on within myself or which path will help me for the day's task or problem. Each card has a corresponding explanation provided for me in a booklet for me to meditate on and help me make sense of my intention. As my intuition and inner guidance grow, I find myself relying less and less on these but do pull them out from time to time.

Angel numbers are numbers that are seen in repetition: 111, 222, 333, etc. These are little reminders that I am not alone, and the Universe is supporting me in my journey. In November 2022, I started seeing these numbers constantly on my phone, sometimes every hour. I just looked, and I have over 60 pictures with the date, including today's 2:22 on 2/22. After some research, I learned that each of these recurring numbers has different meanings. The one that I tend to see the most often and also holds the most meaning for me is 333. Three has been my favorite number for as long as I can remember. My son's birthday is on the 3rd, my daughter's is the 13th, and mine is the 23rd. Seeing the number 333 signifies a powerful and magical number. Most things can be found in groups of three: the birth, death, and rebirth cycle; the past, present, and future; and mind, body, Spirit, to name a few. It is a direct message that is a reminder of my power and Spiritual growth abilities.[51]

In my plant medicine journeys, other than seeing my Soul Sister Cathleen sitting next to me on a tree branch looking down upon the Earth, with the most indescribable bluest eyes and both of us having Angel wings, I had not met or seen my Angel guides until after I did hapé one morning and asked for clearing and healing of my energy. Later that day, suddenly, my ears started ringing loudly, and I took notice and stopped what I was doing. There was a flash of light, I closed my eyes and laid down, and three females appeared. They began healing me by brushing me off, working over me. I started seeing Sacred geometry while they were doing this, I asked them who they were and what their names were. They said they were Angel Guides sent to help me: one was an unnamed female who was shy and didn't speak, one said to call her Pauline, and the other one was called Ava. There are no coincidences in this life, and approximately six months later, I met the sweetest, most sensitive dog named Ava, who became my shadow while I finished writing this book, following me everywhere and sleeping at my feet all day and night. This just shows me that Angels can be both ethereal and in form on this Earth now.

I have always had an uncanny knack for finding coins on the ground. Most often, pennies, wheat ones to be exact, the oldest one being from 1914. My father collected coins, so I

---

51. Lux, H. (n.d.). Good things come in threes: The hidden meaning of Angel number 333. Retrieved on January 2nd, 2023, from: https://www.theangelwriter.com/blog/angel-number-333

am drawn to them, but I have come to realize that they have a greater significance for me. As mentioned earlier, my mom had several miscarriages. One of those, the baby girl right before me, was stillborn. My mom, I believe, was around six months along when she had to give birth to the baby inside of her, knowing that the baby did not have a heartbeat. My sister was laid to rest at the foot of my paternal Grandparents' grave, with a simple flat gravestone etched *Baby*. I have come to know that her name is Penelope, nicknamed Penny, and her Spirit Animal is a lion, the same one that introduced herself to me, Lauren, Lisa, and Cathleen. These pennies that I am finding are reminders that she is with me still. The saying, "Pennies (i.e., Penny's) from Heaven," has never been more appropriate; they signify that they are placed there by her, bringing me good luck and that I am missed.[52]

I also find all different denominations of coins. One day I found four dimes in separate places. I know that sign was from my dad, reminding me he is with me and protecting me. I currently have found 118 wheat pennies in the past 25 years or so. If you break that down numerology-wise: 1+1+8=10, then further to get a single digit, 1+0=1. The number 1 in my own definition means we are all One with each other, One with Spirit; we are all complete and whole, and each unique Souls.

Throughout this healing process, I have learned about the intuitive "clairs" which are associated with the five senses of seeing, feeling, hearing, smelling, and tasting, that are all part of our 6th sense, knowing without proof.[53]

Clairvoyance is seeing. I have experienced a lot of this: Sacred geometry, patterns, codes, pictures, movies playing,

---

52. Luongo, A. (2020). The meaning of finding a Penny: are they Pennies from Heaven? Retrieved on April 2nd, 2022, from: https://www.capecod.com/lifestyle/the-meaning-of-finding-pennies-from-heaven/
53. Rosen, R. (n.d.). Intuition 101: Developing your clairsenses. Retrieved on December 13th, 2022, from: https://www.oprah.com/spirit/developing-your-5-clair-senses-rebecca-rosen

colors, and Valdon's purple eye when in my practice or journey.

Clairsentience is feeling, and as an empath, who is highly attuned to the emotions of others, I can "read" them and understand what they are going through. My problem though, is that I tend to take on their feelings; if someone is happy inside, I am happy. If someone is angry inside, I tend to get angry, and so forth. I have only experienced clairaudience or the ability to *hear* a few times. During a journey in a consulta or immediately following one when I was sleeping, an Angel called out, "Bobby," I was startled awake, and then she said, "You are Loved!" and a golden glow came all over me.

Smelling something is known as clairalience. I can remember certain smells, which can take me back into the past, but I have not yet smelled something that isn't physically there. The same thing goes for clairgustance or tasting something that you haven't necessarily eaten or drank. Although many times I have had this come up for me as an ability to tell someone right away. These last two are experienced as a sign that a deceased loved one is present.

Claircognizance, or clear knowing, by using my instinctual Soul is always a work in progress for me. Sometimes, it is easy to tap into, and other times it is beyond me, as I am generally thinking too much or wanting to know instantly. I have learned to develop my claircognizance the most by working with THEO.[54]

THEO is a group of 12 Archangels that work collectively to deliver their wise teachings and messages. They assist me by helping me remember core Universal truths and Spiritual mysteries that happen outside this human realm of Being, but also in previous and future timelines. THEO and their messages are channeled directly through Sheila Gillette, guided by her husband Marcus, who helps clarify inquiries to them. They never fail to enlighten me, challenging me to answer

---

54. https://asktheo.com/about-theo

my own questions from this place of claircognizance. THEO has taught me how to trust Soul's intuition more and integrate feelings of childhood (orphans) back into Soul as an adult, helping ease the fear of abandonment, unworthiness, and sometimes even death. This allows me to be more present in the here and now and move forward toward the future. I have worked one-on-one with THEO in workshops, programs, and in group settings, and without a doubt, they have been an integral part of Soul's knowing process.

With the guidance of THEO, I also did a lot of inner work around my relationships with men. It started with my daily practice, sitting in my knowingness. What came up from Soul was recognizing that in this lifetime, I was drawn to others from the lower financial energy standpoint of ill-gotten monetary gains. Whether it be my father and his taking bets, my ex-husband, and others misrepresenting themselves with their credentials to gain opportunities, or working for people who weren't entirely truthful in their business practices. These people in my life brought in large sums of money, and in turn, I profited from it, and it helped me feel secure. Only recently did I realize that I am drawn to or align myself with them and tend to stick by them and look the other way in order for me to wish and hope for the big payout partnering with them. This was the unhealthy way Soul attached so quickly to others; the fear of being unlovable and not being able to provide for One's Self financially.

Soul integration started with a releasing of a deep attachment to my father. Spirit visualized my five or six-year-old adoring Self, idolizing him. Bobby loved and cherished him so much, yet she was still clinging to him 50 years later. Due to the timing of his death, which coincided with the separation of marriage and divorce, coupled with the fact that shortly afterward, there was enmeshment with S., Soul was never fully able to grieve his transition. Soul recognized that there was a harmful fairy tale attachment of love, co-dependence, and male role modeling, along with the notion that Bobby needed this type of adoring, being put on a pedestal by a man. Soul needed to be unencumbered by the connection, and so it was done just in the asking, freed with Love and gratitude.

A Spirit-guided, intuitive free writing session was also done in a workshop with THEO. It entailed sitting still after a guided meditation, keeping the eyes closed, and just allowing the pen on the paper or fingers to just freely on the keyboard, quickly typing what intuitively was coming up for Self. Here is what was downloaded, Higher Angelic guidance for sure.

These are teachers for us and lessons learned. Love like a father. Fear of abandonment, inner child wounds of fear. Trust and allow Others to be their own Self, and walk their own path, do Self process, not their own process. Walk Self path, their job to integrate themselves; humans can only provide guidance for when they ask advice. Respect. Be the Light. Self-cord cut with father, ask to start, and restart the relationship with S. establishing better boundaries, can be a bumpy start. No judgment, different vibrations, neither good nor bad. Don't try to analyze or make it personal. It is a matter of knowing what feels right. Be cognizant of that other Self's energy while sleeping and even while miles away. Communicate Soul to Soul, being true and authentic in speech, and what SOUL needs. The other person will energetically feel that, and there will be small vibrational shifts. Cocoon in a bubble without hearing the noise of the outside world. If it was meant to be, it would all be in the Divine timing. There is a plan, a lesson, for both teacher and student. Both Selves are mirrors of what each Self needs to work on. Love; don't doubt it. Soul mates, Soul contracts, or Soul's journey is to incarnate at the same time for a purpose that is Higher Source, not for Self. Be the observer. Breathe, and continue on Self's path if that person is not parallel to the Self. They must walk their own path undisturbed, so don't give up on your Soul's process or path for them. Have mutual reciprocity. Allow their Soul to be heard too and have no fear. Bigger, better, and more expansion will come to Spirit without or without another person. Don't be tethered or entangled unhealthily out of wounding. Be like balloons freely floating in a golden sky, with purple clouds knowing sovereignty. It is hard as a human not to judge but only want the best for them; just by being your best Self, their Soul will see and feel it.

I have never been a dreamer; however, since working with THEO and listening to their meditations right before bed, I have had the most magical, fantastic dreams at night. I started keeping a dream journal by my bed so that first thing in the morning, when I wake up, I can quickly jot them down. There are too many to list here; however, the profound was just recently. Let me explain what happened that night before bed. My partner, S., and I had gone to a housewarming party and was sitting on the couch. A cat came up to both of us, which the owner said was extremely unusual. I am allergic to cats, so I tend to stay away from them. S. never really cared for them; he is more of a dog person. This cat wouldn't stop playing with us and begging for attention. We left the party and went home to sleep. In my dream, I dreamt of cat hair everywhere. It was stuck on blankets, on the floor, on my clothes, and it seemed like it was a lot of work. As I awoke and lay quietly, recalling and wondering about the deeper meaning of this, S. rolled over and said, "I dreamt last night you bought a cat." I was astounded! We had the same dream that night! I asked THEO in my next session with them about it, and they explained that we were both energetically together, connected by a high vibration. Digging even further during one meditation, perhaps what was a lot of work was not the cat hair, which was just symbolic, but the relationship with S.

Present and Past Life Regression

"After thousands and thousands of dreams, we awaken. After thousands and thousands of births, we are born. This, the end, is only the beginning."

—Dr. Brian Weiss

Regression is possible to experience within this lifetime. My Soul Sister Cathleen is a strong intuitive healer that is a Master Facilitator in Regenerating Images in Memory® (RIM). RIM® allows for negative feelings, thoughts, and experiences to be freed within individuals, changing the neural pathways during the process.[55] During my first RIM® healing session, I was exhibiting frustration and a lack of control about something going on in my life. As we spoke remotely over a Zoom call, in her compassionate, loving voice, she asked me when the first time I felt the way I was feeling. I remember back to the time when I was five-years-old, and I was walking with my father in Grant Park, and we came back to the parking lot, only to find out that our car had been stolen. I was frustrated because I had a purple Tootsie Roll Pop in there, and yet exhilarated by the fact I was able to hitchhike with my Dad to get a ride home. Cathleen encouraged me to envision the person that took our car and speak to him like my 5-year-old self. I told him I was mad at him, how dare he ruin a good day, that I wanted my lollipop, and then as my 5-year-old self would do, I promptly gave him a good kick in the shins. Coming out of the session, I immediately started laughing, realizing that I had held that in my body and subconsciousness for a long time and that I could let go of whatever was bothering me present-day and re-imagine it differently. While this story was an easy one for me to re-imagine, RIM® is effective for trauma as well. Cathleen specializes in grief trauma, collaborating with parents and individuals who have lost loved ones unexpectedly.

---

55. https://www.riminstitute.com/the-rim-institute/

My first past life regression was held by my Soul Sister Lisa in a group setting. Lisa is a powerful Shaman who uses many types of journeys for individual awareness to remember past lives. A few days before, I sat in a Kambô and Bufo ceremony and was excited to see what would come through for me; however, as you read this story, you realize that I had not taken any type of medicine during the session. Lisa is a powerful Shaman who uses many types of journeys for individual awareness and remembering. As I lay back on my cot in a circle with the group, listening to her soft, soothing voice, I was immediately and rapidly transported back.

My first past life was with Mother Mushroom. I was a naughty, mischievous fairy playing with my friends in the beautiful woods, and Mother was always chastising me for being too loud, too active, just too much of everything. The wisdom she gave me that I brought into this lifetime was my playfulness. My second life, I was a Native Storyteller, and the Old Wizened Grandmother was tutoring me. I was never really accepted here, others thought of me as a know it all, but due to my title, I was revered. Grandmother gave me the advice of wisdom and the knowledge to teach Others. In the third lifetime, I was Egyptian royalty (much like the story earlier). I was exalted and adored by others in the crowd. I stood in front of the female version of Thoth with an ibis bird: head God of Wisdom, writing, time, and the Moon; perhaps Seshat or Isis. She told me that I was gifted beauty to carry into this world, but being idolized, envied, and jealous of this was to be experienced. In the fourth lifetime, I was reborn as a snake, once again mimicking what I had experienced in my Aya ceremony. Mother Aya, as my snake mother, gave me the gift of courage and strength and the ability to strike when necessary. The lesson was I was never alone, but I could be independent, calling on my internal resources. These gifts would make things difficult as well, for they are often feared, lethal, and considered dangerous in this lifetime. My fifth lifetime, I was in an Angelic realm with my Soul sisters Cathleen and Mother Lisa, who was depicted as someone who looked like Glinda, the good witch from *The Wizard of Oz*. Mother gifted me with my Soul family, my Sisters, and the gift of unconditional Love. While still in the session, I couldn't go back any further into past lives. I asked the Angelic Mother why this was the last life I could remember, and she said that *Love* was the most important gift to carry and remember in this lifetime.

I had one other experience that expounded on my 2nd past life regression in the story above. It was during a THEO-guided session, and I saw myself as an Indigenous (Oceti Sakowin or Sioux, came up for me) female in a field with long black braids. I felt heaviness in my legs, and I realized then that I was not a female but a male. I was picking at plants and studying them, and I realized that not only was I a Storyteller, but that I was also a Medicine Man. I was looking for plants to heal my tribe and teach others how to do so. I saw myself eating these plants, roots, and berries first to see if they would harm me before I gave them to others, as I felt a great responsibility to help, heal and physically save others. A great disease came to the tribe (smallpox, polio?), and no one would listen to me. I was angry because I knew what would help, and I was ashamed of the lack of respect from the people. It was with great sadness and helplessness when I lost many of my friends and family to death. The gift that I brought into this world was that I still get triggered when people are talking or not paying attention to me during lectures, seminars, or even casual conversations. In the past, I was always a rescuer, doer, and saver in this lifetime, always trying to impart my learned knowledge and process to them. These are not driven by ego but passed down from the lifetime of the healer. Many times friends have commented that the snake oil salesman would love me because I am always trying to find the next best cure, remedy, or solution, so it comes full circle for me. This was such a powerful realization.

Both Lisa's and Cathleen's services and contact information are listed under the resource section at the back of this book. I highly recommend them for their gifts and healing services.

PART V:

Wholeness, to be Continued…

Sovereignty

"I am in this world; Soul is not of this world."

—*Me*

"There is a supreme power and ruling force which pervades and rules the boundless Universe. You are a part of this power."

—*Prentice Mulford*

It was when I was at a 10-day silent retreat during one of our eight one-hour meditations for the day that I had a vision of myself as an Egyptian Goddess. I remember lounging in an open-air palanquin[1] or carrying chair, lifted with poles by four men and being carefully let down in front of an audience before being presented with a single white rose. I remember being crowned and being treated like royalty, adored, admired, and loved. Sovereignty is the "defining authority within individual consciousness."[2] While I did not recognize it at the time, this was the first remembrance of past Sovereignty, Divine Goddess feminine, and part of Soul Bobby. Shortly after this vision, I also found my literal voice during this retreat. I remember walking down to the ocean, wanting to scream out loud at it and not being able to get the scream

---

1. Palanquins were only used by highly esteemed individuals and royalty for transportation in ancient Egypt (2780-1650 B.C.). Ancient Egyptian land transportation: Foot travel, roads, chariots, and carts. *Ancient Egyptian transportation.* (n.d.). Retrieved on February 12th, 2023, from: https://factsanddetails.com/world/cat56/sub404/item1928.html#chapter-2
2. Retrieved on January 30th, 2023, from: https://en.wikipedia.org/wiki/Sovereignty

out. No one was around, but I couldn't manage more than a squeak. I cried and turned back to go journal in my room. That night, I had a dream of having a crown on my head, stepping into Sovereignty as was my Soul's birthright here on Earth. The next morning, I woke up, walked down to the ocean once again, and let out several loud screams at the top of my lungs. As the Queen that I am, I would not, could not be silenced or quiet any longer.

Soul Remembrance

> "I am the coming together of all quantized fields of the Universe appearing in a form your feeble human brain can comprehend."
>
> —*Jerry*[3]

> "There is no I, no me or my, no ego, no separation, only Soul knowing and remembrance."
>
> —*Me*

I am so grateful to have received so many healing boons over these last few years: finding my way back to Soul, shedding my ego, my shame, my caretaking of others, getting back to Light and Love, returning to the Spiritual realm and to Spirit. As you have read thus far, I have achieved this through plant and animal medicine, various cord-cutting techniques, modalities of calling back and retrieving Soul fragments, inner child and shadow work, and the various other practices I've curated in my toolkit. But it is a remembering what I was gifted as I continue to live a Soul driven life.

I feel like I was too late to remember all of this. I was 42 years old when I started this quest; 54–57 years old was the

---

3. Jerry is a collective of Universal consciousness in the movie *Soul*. Docter, P. (Director). (2020). *Soul* [Film]. Pixar Animation Studios for Walt Disney Pictures.

most demanding part. Some people I know have started their journey in their 30s or even 20s, and they are the lucky Ones. But I am not bitter, just pensive. I also realize that some do not ever start rescuing Soul in this lifetime. While re-reading my all-time favorite book, *Women Who Run with the Wolves* (1992),[4] by Dr. Clarissa Pinkola Estés, I realized that even though I started at the seeker state midway through this human life, Soul remembrance was right on schedule. In an effort to break down this learning into a woman's chronological framework, Dr. Estés depicts it like this:

"0–7   *age of the body and dreaming/socialization yet retaining imagination*
7–14   *age of separating yet weaving together reason and the imaginal*
14–21   *age of new body/young maidenhood/unfurling yet protecting sensuality*
21–28   *age of new world/new life/exploring the woods*
28–35   *age of the mother/learning to mother self/ seeking the self*
35–42   *age of the seeker/learning to mother others and self*
41–49   *age of the early crone/finding the far encampment/giving courage to others*
49–56   *age of the underworld/learning the words and rites*
56–63   *age of choices/choosing one's world and the work yet to be done*
63–70   *age of becoming watchwoman/recasting all one has learned*
70–77   *age of re-youthanization/more cronedom*
77–84   *age of the mist beings/finding more big in the small*
84–91   *age of weaving with the scarlet thread/understanding the weaving of life*

---

4. https://www.amazon.com/Women-Who-Run-Wolves-Archetype/dp/0345409876/

91–98   *age of the ethereal/less to saying, more to being*
98–105 *age of pneuma, the breath*
105 +   *age of timelessness"* (p.p. 484–485)[5]

Intuition

> "Thoughts in my mind are just thoughts and stories but knowings that come up in Soul, are important intuitions. Feel into these."
>
> —Me

To be able to say I am intuitive means that I ask myself many questions. *What does Soul want? What is Soul hungry for? What does Soul need? What does Bobby wish for? What best suits Soul? How does Bobby feel? Does this serve Soul's highest and best purpose?* These answers have to come from deep inside Soul, a knowing, without being presented with options to choose from. One of the hardest intuitive decisions I recently had to make was not to experience Iboga or San Pedro with Soul Sisters. I had major FOMO (fear of missing out), but even without considering or thinking about it, Spirit said, "Not interested." There were also many rational thoughts about why I couldn't go with them, but my gut feeling was an immediate "no." Anytime I ever felt repression of Soul, thoughts or ideas or felt pressured to make a decision, nine times out of ten, I went against my innate sense of what Soul wanted. Society, family, friends, or fear will never again be a reason to agree or disagree with what is best for me. I chose only to listen to Soul.

Just this past month, out of the blue, I received a guided intuitive message from a THEO group member, Mark Chabus.[6]

---
5. Estés, C. (1992). *Women Who Run with the Wolves*. Random House Publishing.
6. https://www.markchabus.com/

"Bobby—I know why you're here and what you came to do. Not specifically, because that's really your choice and not a requirement. But you're a leader, a healer, a teacher, and a way shower. How can I help you to advance in a way that is in alignment with that and in a way that you choose? I have a message for you, and it's about remembering. Even though I wrote a book about that, it's never been a message for anyone else specifically but you. Remember- that's your calling. Like the phone that keeps on ringing, we're too busy to answer, but it's hard to concentrate on anything else. I can't imagine a phone that is always ringing- sometimes loudly, sometimes faintly, but always, always there.

In a second message from Mark, I received this:

"You are VERY intuitive. It's all about trusting the Source. It's funny because the info will come, but then we are like, did I just make that up? Ha-ha. The truth is we doubt because of the way we were conditioned from birth. We are taught that everything has to be "outside" of us. We always surrender our own authority to someone that seems more qualified or connected. Believe me; I was the king of this. But then, one day, we wake up and we see the ridiculousness of all of it. The authority is you, and when you wake up to that, you immediately remember you are making all of this up. You are the creator! You make up the body, you make up the signs, and you make up the person you need to tell you those signs are real. If you accept that, the old self collapses, and you become what you always were meant to be an incredibly powerful, wise, loving, compassionate, creative being free to be your authentic Self and enjoy the sh*t out of this incredible journey called life."

Perfectly said.

Life Not Yet Lived and Choosing

> "It is not our circumstances, our family, friends, money, or occupation that make the quality of this Life rewarding and joyous. It is the choices we make when we are guided by Soul."
>
> —Me

Just like in one of my journeys, seeing the Book of Life and asking about the empty pages, I cannot yet write this next section completely, so therefore, it is brief.

The question now Soul always asks is, how can I be the best Bobby in service with the gifts I have gained and received for the Highest good for myself and all others?

I just had an Akashic record reading done about my healing gifts in this lifetime by Merryman Cassels,[7] and she shared the following: I am meant to teach healers, 'heal the healer' as it was written. My gifts are to serve with the highest *integrity* possible, create a new structure and process, blending the gifts of my business skills (bulleted steps, action, creation, vision) that already have been developed with my newly acquired awareness. But I need to start with the vision and work backward, opposite of what I am used to doing, to develop an instructed format to serve. I am stepping into my purpose as being a thought leader, an open channel, creating a safe container for others, to inform, and take this new paradigm, shared from Source to a globally scaled audience of healers. I will share this in a compassionate, authentic way, while listening to others' needs to make their lives or businesses more orderly, more manageable by helping remove barriers of limiting beliefs. *There is not a sea so deep that I can't swim in it, not a sky so high that I can't fly in it.*

So, I choose to take Soul friends and family back, my time and energy back, my physical body back, my passion back, but most of all, I am taking my Sovereignty back. I

---

7. https://www.merrymancassels.com/

refuse to be contained, blocked or absorb others' lower vibration energy. I will not disregard my intuition and will rely on every little nuance, feeling, and emotion within myself. I deserve Divine flow in this life. I will tend to Soul first and foremost. I will not acquiesce, be quieted, or be boxed in if it goes against Soul; I will fight lovingly and escape inwardly to become free. I choose not only to survive but to thrive in co-creation with other like-minded Beings. I will no longer think in terms of "what ifs" or fantasies of what could become, but I will recognize the signs: repeating numbers, ringing within my ears to stop and listen to Soul. I will know that finding wheat pennies signifies Spirit guides are always nearby. While looking to grow and travel, I will stay open to new dimensional portals to help guide Soul on my intentional path effortlessly. I will no longer force, beg, or freely give away Soul's Light so that it becomes dim. Rather, Soul giving will be effortless, heart-centered, radiating Love back into this world. There will be an ebbing and a flowing of reciprocal giving and receiving. Soul will regain focus with the passion of the human life's purpose, resting and playing (not working manically) as needed. All guidance is within. I will continue to access Soul deep listening while continuing the work to claim back the disparate parts of Self.

I choose to hold out for what best serves the highest Spirit, relationships, purpose, health, and passions. Traveling, water, fun and play, Higher Spiritual knowledge, creating and teaching, quiet time in meditation, dreaming and journeying, and nourishing food are Soul's form of Self Love. I will walk with my head held high, knowing I am learning to rediscover Soul and therefore, seeking to find Others on this Earth that have done their work as well. Soul dropped the luggage of trauma, and Spirit is now flying with dragon's wings into a new chapter of this life. Soul is finally breathing again. Big, full, with beautiful bountiful breaths of air, no longer constricted by what others think of Bobby. Not trying to save anyone, not feeling shame or anger, just walking this path with happiness, Love, and gratitude. Bobby is not willing to walk any longer in a continuous cycle of repetition, but she is going to continue to allow healing and new creation to take place. This new Bobby remembers her lost Spirit, Soul knowledge, and has regained Spiritual fire. She knows the wholeness of Being, unconditional Soul Love, Light of Spirit, the service of life's Purpose, and that Soul is everlasting. It is a remembering of the infinite wisdom of Soul.

Acknowledgements

The inspiration to write this book was to help *anyone* that was curious, needed insight, options, or healing. If this story can help one person on a deeper inner journey to release trauma and receive awareness, then my Soul's purpose in this lifetime has been fulfilled. If it can help a hundred or more, even more so!

To my children: JR and Kyra, I love you both so much!

Thank you to my three biological brothers: Jim, Jon, and Mike. You bring such joy, happiness, laughter, and gratitude to life. I am so fortunate that we chose to be born to be together. I love you.

To my sister and the numerous other Soul siblings that did not materialize here on Earth, thank you for being my guides with this process. I feel you.

Also, I am in such deep, profound gratitude to:

Soul Sisters—Cathleen, Lisa, Ellen, and Lauren. There are no words, and we don't need any.

Soul Brothers—Brant, Gerry P., and Roark. Keep on the Soul path; you all make this world a better, brighter place with your Love and Light. I strive to speak the same language.

Soul and Medicine Family—Gerry A. P., Carlos, Luis, Brad, Sara, Luis, Leo, Shams, Jocelyn, Raven, Karina, Nikko, Marcus, Sheila, Mark C., Agris, thank you for walking the path of healing and awareness within yourself and helping Others with this as well. I am One with you.

Spiritual Teachers—Deepak, Taita Juanito, Taita Luis, and THEO, your gifts of knowledge and healing have helped me tremendously. I see your widespread energy and superpowers.

Plant and Animal Medicine—Thank you for connecting me back to Soul. I remember.

Mentors and Academics—Dr. John M., Jack C., and any others I have forgotten to mention, thank you for all your help, teaching me how to tackle the research on non-traditional modalities, practices, and the benefits and effects of medicines on this human body. Jack, thank you for encouraging me to step into my greatness, and add substance and credibility to my experiences, journeys, and visions received. I know you.

Adversaries and Supporters—There is Yin/Yang, darkness/light, non-benevolent/benevolent, sadness/happiness, low energy vibrations/high energy vibrations all around. Learn to embrace both, for each of these is just a reflection of Soul, and the uncomfortableness with one is the inner work still needed. Thank you for the lessons both have provided. I am in flow.

Kate, my publisher, and her dream team at Butler Books, Kristy, my hawk-eyed editor, Michelle, my book designer, and the early readers of this book—thank you for your help getting this book off the shelves and into the hands of the perfect person in Divine Kairos timing. I trust in the process.

About the Author

Roberta (Bobby) Pellant is a Professor, Consultant, Entrepreneur, #1 International Best-Selling co-author of *Women Who Empower*, and Keynote Speaker on a Soul driven mission, looking to transform leaders, one business at a time.

Bobby has 25 + years teaching as a Professor, including international lecturing in management, marketing, human resources, and communication. Additionally, Roberta Pellant is an accredited leadership coach and holds a certification as a cultural assessment practitioner from the Barrett Values Centre.

She is a successful entrepreneur, owner of Roberta Pellant Consulting, working with both small business owners and C-level executives and their teams to transform, inspire, and motivate them to help them meet their professional needs. She focuses on three key areas: one-on-one executive coaching and consulting, professional development training, and motivational speaking. Customized offerings are highly interactive and include actionable recommendations to apply immediately. Bobby is considered a top business expert across all industries, and has been featured on ABC Chronicle, Jack Canfield's Success TV show, and in Wall Street Select, Yahoo! Finance, Market Watch, and International Business.

Bobby is also the founder of The Business Success Institute, which was developed as a holistic, compassionate way of doing business, focusing on building meaningful relationships and fostering a heart-centered approach to business. The Institute is committed to fostering an environment of collaboration, trust, and authenticity. Their coaching and consulting philosophy is grounded in the belief that by supporting individuals in achieving their personal and professional goals, they can create a positive ripple effect that extends far beyond the workplace. The team is dedicated to providing unparalleled support and expertise to their clients. They are passionate about helping their clients achieve their most daring goals and create a future that's more fulfilling than they ever thought possible.

Bobby's TEDx talk, "I Want You to Fail," highlights her powerful speaking abilities and unique perspective on overcoming fear in the pursuit of business success and fear of failing on a personal level. Her dynamic presence and compelling insights continue to inspire and empower audiences.

Bobby lives in Hingham, MA. She enjoys golfing, listening to the rain, playing cards, reading, and especially walking on the beach, finding sea glass. She is the mother of two adult children, J.R. and Kyra.

Bobby is available for, but not limited to, keynote speaking, panel discussions, 90-minute sessions, full-day workshops, webinars, or multi-tiered events. For speaking inquiries or to learn more about Bobby's work, please visit: www.robertapellant.com and https://www.linkedin.com/in/bobbypellant/

Resources

Lisa Bryer

Lisa Wray Bryer is a certified past life regression guide, reiki master, intuitive, spirit guide messenger, and Shamanic healing practitioner with a deep commitment to spiritual growth and healing. Her journey began mid-life when she sought answers to life's questions through past life regression. This experience led her to recognize the transformative power of the unseen world as a guide in this world.

With extensive training in Shamanic healing and intuitive practices, Lisa is skilled in weaving together a wide range of modalities to provide her clients with a holistic and personalized approach to healing. Her involvement with plant and amphibian medicine has opened up her heart and expanded her awareness of other dimensions, allowing her to provide profound insights and support to others on their healing journey. Lisa is a compassionate guide who helps individuals overcome barriers in their lives, whether through past life exploration or addressing issues that are holding them back in their current life. She is a mother of two grown children and resides in Rhode Island with her husband Jim and their beloved Tennessee Covid-pup, Maisie. If you would like to connect with Lisa, you can reach her at: angelwrays@gmail.com.

Cathleen Elle

Cathleen Elle is a transformational speaker, certified master coach and healer, visionary guide for sudden loss, and an award-winning author. Her book, *Shattered Together: A Mother's Journey From Grief to Belief*, is a practical guide for those struggling with loss of any kind and has become a #1 international bestseller on Amazon. Cathleen's journey with plant medicines has been a significant part of her life, supporting her own healing and transformation, and now incorporating them in her work as a guide. After experiencing the tragic loss of her son to suicide, Cathleen uncovered a powerful sense of self and a connection to the divine that motivated her to redesign her life and help others do the same. Today, she specializes in Regenerating Images in Memory (RIM), a multi-sensory technique that facilitates mental, physical, and spiritual transformation. Cathleen provides personalized one-on-one support, virtual and in-person group sessions, and transformative retreats to parents who have experienced loss. She is also available as a speaker, inspiring audiences on topics such as suicide prevention, grief, and self-discovery. To learn more about her work and book a session visit: Cathleenelle.com or email cathleen@cathleenelle.com.

Lauren Greenlee

Lauren has been the events director for large and small-scale events, retreats, festivals, and conferences across multiple countries in Southeast Asia, the United Kingdom and Central and North America. She has organized events with global brands, embassies, spiritual retreat centers and multiple-day music festivals with over 20,000 attendees. She has been blessed with the opportunity in this lifetime to navigate her healing and spiritual journey alongside Bobby, which has kept her grounded in the world of event planning. Lauren is currently residing in the United States and is open to organizing new events around the world. Her email is laurengreenlee.events@gmail.com

Ellen Plamp

Ellen Plamp is a reiki master, healing touch practitioner, medical intuitive, certified plant medicine integration coach, and animal communicator. Ellen's background in Nursing spans over 40 years. Her specialty for 20 of those years was in Mental Health and Hospice until she retired in 2020. She has been practicing since 1996, working within the physical and energetic body of her clients to assess their energetic field for blockages and imbalances to bring the energetic flow back to balance and harmony. As a holistic energetic practitioner, she utilizes a wide range of modalities combined with a channeled healing method that Ellen has been working with since 2018. She has facilitated thousands of sessions with the intention of assisting her clients on their journey to self-healing and empowerment as well as deepening their understanding of their own intuitive abilities. Ellen currently resides in Tampa, Florida, and provides both in-person and remote quantum healing sessions with her clients, as well as mentoring and integration coaching pre- and post-plant medicine experiences. She can be contacted at: Quantumhealingintegration@gmail.com.

Mark Chabus

Mark Chabus is a life coach, intuitive, and author. He was trained as a coach by well-known self-help expert Tony Robbins, as well as world renowned psychotherapist Cloe Madanes. Mark has a BS in Psychology from the State University of New York, College at Oneonta as well as a degree in Classic Culinary Arts from the French Culinary Institute. Chabus' leadership and speaker training is from Harvard University. After a successful, two-decade-long career in the NYC catering and event industry, Chabus shifted gears. He now focuses on spreading his messages about emotional intelligence, positive thinking, spiritual awareness, and how to turn pain into opportunities for strength and growth. The wisdom he imparts is the result of his experiences after losing his girlfriend in the Twin Towers on 9/11. He is the author of *Remembering Your Spirit* and co-host of the *This is Source* podcast. Chabus currently resides in a suburb of North Carolina with his wife, Kate, and their four children, ages ten, seven, five, and three. To work with Mark, please visit https://www.markchabus.com/ or email him at markchabus@gmail.com.

www.ingramcontent.com/pod-product-compliance
Lightning Source LLC
Chambersburg PA
CBHW041324110526
44592CB00021B/2807